An Exploration of the SARFAESI Act

This book looks at the constitutional and regulatory frameworks of loan and debt recovery laws and legislations. It explores different aspects of the Securitisation and Reconstruction of Financial Assets and Enforcement of Security Interest (SARFAESI) Act, 2002, along with the issues and challenges in enforcing the Act in India.

The book explores the evolution of debt recovery laws in India by analysing various past cases and legislations relating to the recovery of dues by banks and financial institutions. Taking the rights of both banks and borrowers into consideration, it provides a description of the relevant provisions of the SARFAESI Act and its implications. The author analyses relevant case laws and practical experiences to highlight the positives and the issues of the SARFAESI Act that have strengthened the creditor's rights in India. The book also looks at the consolidation of insolvency and bankruptcy laws in India that have contributed to the process of debt recovery while protecting customers.

Lucid and comprehensive, this volume will be an indispensable resource for students and researchers of law, business and company law, monetary economics, macroeconomics, Asian law, and comparative law. It will also be useful for teaching faculty, legal practitioners and bankers.

Syamjith Parakkott has 27 years of experience in banking law and practice. At present, he is serving as the chief manager in the law department of the State Bank of India, Thiruvananthapuram, India. He has authored several books and articles on banking laws and has participated in many seminars and workshops as a resource person.

An Exploration of the SARFAESI Act

Practical Insights

Syamjith Parakkott

Routledge
Taylor & Francis Group
LONDON AND NEW YORK

First published 2025
by Routledge
4 Park Square, Milton Park, Abingdon, Oxon OX14 4RN

and by Routledge
605 Third Avenue, New York, NY 10158

Routledge is an imprint of the Taylor & Francis Group, an informa business

British Library Cataloguing-in-Publication Data
A catalogue record for this book is available from the British Library

ISBN: 978-1-032-37360-7 (hbk)
ISBN: 978-1-032-90118-3 (pbk)
ISBN: 978-1-003-54623-8 (ebk)

DOI: 10.4324/9781003546238

Typeset in Sabon
by Apex CoVantage, LLC

Dedicated to my parents, teachers, wife, children and other family members.

Contents

List of figures *viii*
List of tables *ix*
List of cases *x*
Foreword *xvi*
Preface *xvii*
Acknowledgements *xix*

1 An exploration of the SARFAESI Act – practical insights 1

2 The evolution and development of recovery laws relating to banks and financial institutions 6

3 The constitutional and regulatory frameworks of recovery laws relating to banks and financial institutions 16

4 Legislations relating to the recovery of dues to banks in force in India 47

5 The role of judiciary in interpreting and establishing recovery laws relating to banking institutions 73

6 The issues and challenges in enforcing the SARFAESI Act, 2002 108

7 The Insolvency and Bankruptcy Code, 2016: A big game changer in banking! 117

8 Implications of the SARFAESI Act on various systems 125

Bibliography *134*
Index *140*

Figures

2.1	Stages of the concept of recovery of dues	7
2.2	Pyramid chart – the evolution of banking recovery laws through various stages	8
4.1	Pictorial representation of the four dimensions of the SARFAESI Act	59
8.1	Pictorial representation of the effects of the SARFAESI Act on various systems	126
8.2	Pictorial representation of the effects of the SARFAESI Act on the social system	129
8.3	Pictorial representation of the effects of the SARFAESI Act on the legal system	131
8.4	Pictorial representation of the effects of the SARFAESI Act on the banking system	133

Tables

3.1 Original definition of NPA as given under the provisions of the SARFAESI Act, 2002, and the amended definition of NPA after the Amendment Act passed in 2004. 26
3.2 Comparison of the provisions before and after the SARFAESI Amendment Act. 42
3.3 Comparison of the provisions before and after the DRT Amendment Act. 45

Cases

A

Allahabad Bank v. Canara Bank and Another, AIR 2000 SC 1535, 2000(4) SCC 406. 21, 46n6.

Allahabad Bank v. Radha Krishna Maity, (1999) 6 SCC 755. 32, 46n16.

Assam Leather Industry v. Union of India (UOI) and Others on August 16, 1999: 2001 104 CompCas 115 Gauhati/Indian Kanoon – http://indiankanoon.org/doc/1237648/. 17, 46n2.

Authorised Officer, Indian Overseas Bank and Another v. Ashok Saw Mill reported in 2009(2) D.R.T.C.545 (S.C.). 80–81.

B

Bajarang Shyamsunder Agarwal v. Central Bank of India & Another, Criminal Appeal No. 1371/2019. 99–100.

Bank of India v. Barry Sebastian, 2013(1) KHC 584. 71, 72n5.

Bank of Maharashtra Ltd v. Official Liquidator, High Court Buildings, AIR 1969 Mys. 280. 46n29.

C

Cham Trading Organisation and Others v. Authorised Officer and Chief Manager Bank of Baroda, Ahmedabad, 2010(1) Bank CLR 594 (DRAT Mum). 95–96, 107n19.

City and Industrial Development Corporation v. Dosu Aardeshir Bhiwandiwala and Others, (2009) 1 SCC 168. 83, 106n8.

Collector of Customs, Madras v. Nathella Sampathu reported in 1962(3) SCR 786 at pp. 829–30. 106n3.

D

Dahya Lal v. Rasul Mohd. Abdul Rahim, (1963) 3 SCR. 35, 46n22.
Decan Chronicles Holdings Limited v. Union of India and Others, W.P.No.5897/2014. 28, 46n13.
Delhi High Court Bar Association and Another v. Union of India and Others reported in AIR 1995 Delhi 323. 16, 46n1.
Dharani Sugars and Chemicals Ltd v. Union of India & Others, Transferred Case (Civil) No.66/2018. 124n2.
D.J. Exim (India) Pvt. Ltd & Others v. State Bank of India & Others, Writ Petition (L) No.2808 of 2013. 116n3.
D.K. Abdul Khader and Others v. Union of India and Others reported in AIR 2001 Kant 179. 17, 46n5.

E

Eureka Forbes Limited v. Allahabad Bank and Others, Civil Appeal No.4029 of 2010 (Arising out of SLP © No.3883 of 2008). 84–85, 106n9.

G

Ganga Bai v. Vijay Kumar, (1974) 2 SCC 393. 33, 46n18.

H

Harshad Govardhan Sondagar v. International Assets Reconstruction Co. Ltd & Others, Criminal Appeal No.736 of 2014. 100, 109, 116n2.

I

ICICI Bank v. Shanti Devi Sharma and Others, 2008(2) Bank CLR 745 (SC). 86–87, 106n11.
Indian Bank v. Blue Jaggers Estates Ltd and Others reported in 2010(4) Current Tamil Nadu Cases (SC). 85–86, 106n10.
Indian Bank v. M/s. Nippon Enterprises South, AIR 2011 Madras 230. 108, 116n1.
Indian Overseas Bank v. Sree Aravindh Steels Ltd, 2009(1) CTC 341 (DB). 111, 116n4.

International Asset Reconstruction Company Private Ltd v. Union of India and Others, Crl. Public Interest Litigation No.24 of 2011. 113, 116n12.

ITO v. Mohd Kunhi, (1969) 2 SCR 65. 32, 46n15.

J

J. Malliga and Others v. Authorized Officer, Union Bank of India, Regional Office, Madurai, (2010) 4 MLJ. 93–94, 106n17.

J. Rajiv Subramaniyan & Another v. M/s. Pandiyas & Others, Civil Appeal No.3866/2014, S.L.P© No.25448/2012. 115, 116n15.

Jabbar and Another v. Dhanalakshmi Bank Ltd. and Others, 2005 KHC 898. 71, 72n6.

Jain and Co v. Capital First Ltd & Others, Civil Appeal No.175/2022. 116n7.

Jagdish Singh v. Heeralal and Others, Civil Appeal No.9771/2013 (Arising out of Special Leave Petition (Civil) No.18 of 2011). 111, 116n8.

Jupiter Jewel Tech represented by Its Partners & Others v. Authorised Officer, Indian Overseas Bank, Chennai, 2010(1) D.R.C.714 (Mad). 96–97, 107n20.

K

K. Abdul Khader and Others v. Union of India and Others reported in AIR 2001 Kant 179. 46n3.

K. Arockiyaraj v. The Chief Judicial Magistrate, Srivilliputhur, Virudhunagar District, 2013(5) CTC 15. 111, 116n6.

K. Sreedhar v. M/s. Raus Constructions Pvt. Ltd., and Others, Civil Appeal Nos.7402/2022, SLP 9 (Civil) No.7402/2022, SLP (Civil) No.14695/2020. 103–104.

K. Virupaksha & Another v. The State of Karnataka & Another, Criminal Appeal No.377/2020. 105.

Kamal Gupta and etc. v. Bank of India and Another, 2008(2) Bank CLR 369 (Del). 91–92, 106n14.

Kanshi Ram v. Lachhman, (2001) 5 SCC 546. 35, 46n23.

Keshavlal Khemchand and Sons Pvt. Ltd v. Union of India and Others, Writ Petition (Civil) No.901 of 2014. 26, 46n12.

Kishanchand Arora v. Commissioner of Police reported in 1961(3) SCR 135. 77, 106n4.

Kotak Mahindra Bank Ltd. v. Dilip Bhosale Special Leave to Appeal (C) No(s). 13241–13242/2019. 98, 105–106, 107n22.

Kotak Mahindra Bank Pvt. Ltd v. Ambuj A. Kasliwal & Others, Civil Appeal No.538 of 2021. 105.

Kottakkal Co-operative Urban Bank v. T. Balakrishnan & Others, AIR 2008 Kerala 179. 89–91, 106n13.

L

L and T Finance Limited. v. State of Maharashtra and Another. . . . Respondents. Civil Appeal No.175 of 2022. 102–103.
L. Chandrakumar v. Union of India, (1997) 3 SCC 261. 46n24.
Lakshmi Shankar Mills (P) Ltd. & Others v. Authorised Officer/Chief Manager, Indian Bank & Others, etc., AIR 2008 Madras 181. 88–89, 106n12.

M

Madhu Sudan Ghosh & Others v. the Bank of Baroda & Others, reported in MANU/WB/0349/2010. 99.
Mardia Chemicals v. Union of India, (2004) 4 SCC 311. 13, 15n7.
Mardia Chemicals Ltd v. Union of India, AIR 2004 SC 2371. 46n27.
Mathew Varghese v. M. Amritha Kumar and Others, MANU/SC/0114/2014, Civil Appeal Nos.1927–1929 of 2014. 114, 116n13.
Mercury Exporters and Manufacturing Pvt. Ltd & Another v. Punjab National Bank and Another, W.P.No.353 of 2014. 32, 46n17.
M/s. Kanchee Fashion Sarees & Others v. Authorised Officer, SBI, Kancheepuram & Others, dated 20 February 2014. 113–114, 116n15.
M/S Kannu Aditya India Ltd. vs State Bank of India on 26 October, 2018 (indiankanoon.org) 99
Muhammed Asharaf v. Union of India, AIR 2009 Ker 14. 111, 116n5.

N

NKGSB Co-operative Bank Ltd. v. Subir Chakravarty & Others, S.L.P. (Civil) No.30240 of 2019. 104–105.

O

Omeshwar Baldwa v. Vasavi Co-operative Urban Bank Ltd, 2010(1) Bank CLR 680 (AP). 94–95, 107n18.

P

Phoenix ARC Private Limited v. Vishwa Bharati Vidya Mandir & Others, Civil Appeal Nos.257–259 of 2022. 98, 107n23.

Punjab National Bank, Dasuya v. Chajju Ram and Others, AIR 2000 SC 2671. 23, 46n7.
Purnea Cold Storage v. SBI, Authorised Officer, SAMB, Patna C.W.J.C.No.8746 of 2012. 112.

R

Ramaswamy Aiyengar v. Kailasa Thevar, 1951 SCR 292. 35, 46n21.
Ram Murty Pyara Lal and others v. Central Bank of India and Others, 2010(1) Bank CLR 70 (DRAT). 93, 106n16.
R.D. Jain and Co. v. Capital First Ltd. & Others, High Court of Jammu & Kashmir WP(C) No.465/2021R.D. 111, 116n7.

S

S. Karthik & Others v. N. Subhash Chand Jain and Others, Civil Appeal No.5920–5923/2021. 103.
Sama Rubbers represented by Its Managing Partner v. South Indian Bank Ltd and Others, OP (DRT) No.392 of 2023. 104.
Saraspathy Sundararaj Proprietrix v. Authorised Officer and Assistant General Manager, State Bank of India, SARB, Chennai, CDJ 2010 MHC 5284-W.P.No.15146 of 2010 & M.P.No.1 of 2010. 97–99, 107n21.
S.K. Bakshi v. Punjab National Bank and Others/Respondent(s), SC CM No.4507/2021. 102.
Sondagar v. International Assets Reconstruction Co. Ltd & Others, Criminal Appeal No.736/14, S.L.P (Crl.) No.1666/12. 107n25.
Standard Chartered Bank v. Applitech Solution Ltd & Others, AIR 2009 Gujarat 54. 92–93, 106n15.
Standard Chartered Bank v. Noble Kumar & Others, Criminal Appeal No.1218 of 2013. 102, 112, 116n11.
Surinder Pal Singh v. Vijaya Bank & Others, Civil Appeal No.6843/2023. 103.
Surya Dev Rai v. Ram Chander Rai, (2003) 6 SCC 675. 46n25.

T

Transcore v. Union of India & An Appeal (Civil) No.3228 of 2006. 72n2, 72n3.
Transcore v. Union of India and Another, AIR 2007 SC 712, MANU/SC/5319/2006. 73, 78, 106n2, 106n5, 112, 116n10, 130.
Tirupati Storage and Allied Pvt Ltd. v. the United Commercial Bank, Kolkata, reported in 2012 (4) PLJR 748. 99.

U

Union of India and Another v. Delhi High Court Bar Association and Others reported in AIR 2002 SC 1479, 2002(2) SCR 450, 2002(4) SCC 275. 18, 46n4.
Union of India v. Delhi High Court Bar Association, AIR 2002 SC 1479. 12, 15n6.
United Bank of India v. Satyawati Tondon and Others arising out of SLP© No.10145 of 2010. 15n8, 82–84, 98, 105, 106n7.

V

V. Narasimhachariar v. Egmore Benefit Society, 3rd Branch Ltd., AIR 1955 Mad. 135. 135 46n28.
V.P. Padmavati v. P.S. Swaminathan Iyer, AIR 1955 Mad. 343 (sic). 46n28.
Vishal N. Kalsaria v. Bank of India and Others, AIR 2016 Supreme Court 530. 100–101, 107n26.

W

W.T. Commr., A.P v. Court of Wards, Paigah AIR 1977 SC. 94.

Foreword

The relevance and utility of a legislative enactment can reasonably be discerned when law reports are replete with judicial pronouncements interpreting its various provisions and when it simultaneously remains a topic of serious discussion in circles beyond the realm of law.

The Securitisation and Reconstruction of Financial Assets and Enforcement of Security Interest Act, 2002, commonly known as the SARFAESI Act, is one such statute that has, for more than two decades since its enactment, engaged the serious attention of both legally trained minds and the general public.

As a tool of social engineering devised to meet the necessities of our times, the SARFAESI Act has been both lauded and criticised. It has been subjected to close scrutiny not only by judges, lawyers and legal academics, but also by other stakeholders, including bankers and professionals from the fiscal and monetary fields.

The book at hand is a treatise authored by someone whose expertise spans both the legal field and the realm of banking. This book is a scholarly addition to the wealth of academic study available on the subject. What sets this book apart is the unique approach the author takes in examining the subject from the practical viewpoint of a banker, which is a refreshing change from the usual pedantic legal discussions. That the author has, in respective chapters, attempted to analyse the jurisprudence behind the debt recovery legislations and further proceeded to carry out a doctrinal study based on the judicial precedents as to deduce the approach of courts to SARFAESI Act is a commendable exercise worth special mention.

I congratulate Dr. Syamjith Parakkott for this stupendous effort and wish him all success in his future academic pursuits.

4th June 2024
Justice Viju Abraham
Judge of High Court of Kerala

Preface

The Securitisation and Reconstruction of Financial Assets and Enforcement of Security Interest Act, 2002, was enacted with the intention to strengthen the creditors' rights through foreclosure and enforcement of securities by the banks and financial institutions by conferring on the creditors the right to seize and sell the secured assets in order to recover dues promptly and bypass the costly and time-consuming legal court process.

The statements of objectives and reasons in itself declare that our existing legal framework in India relating to commercial transactions has not kept pace with the changing commercial practices and financial sector reforms, which has resulted in a slow pace of recovery of defaulting loans and the mounting levels of non-performing assets of banks and financial institutions. The Narasimham Committees I and II and the Andhyarujna Committee constituted by the Central Government for the purpose of examining banking sector reforms have considered the need for changes in the legal system in respect to these areas. These committees, *inter alia*, have suggested enactment of a new legislation for securitisation and to empower banks and financial institutions to take possession of the securities and sell them without the intervention of the court. Acting on these suggestions, the Securitisation and Reconstruction of Financial Assets and Enforcement of Security Interest Ordinance, 2002, was promulgated by the Central Government on 21st June 2002 to regulate securitisation and reconstruction of financial assets and enforcement of security interest and for matters connected therewith or incidental thereto. The ordinance received the assent of the president and became an Act. The Act, in effect, enabled banks and financial institutions to realise long-term assets, manage problem of liquidity and asset liability mismatches and improve recovery by exercising powers to take possession and sell securities and reduce non-performing assets by adopting measures for recovery or reconstruction.

A humble attempt has been made here to prepare a comprehensive book on SARFAESI Act and its procedures with special reference to the banks in India. In this book, the evolution and development of recovery laws relating to banks and financial institutions, constitutional and regulatory frameworks of recovery laws relating to banks and financial institutions, legislations relating to recovery of dues to banks in India, issues and challenges in enforcing the SARFAESI Act, the Insolvency and Bankruptcy Code and the implications of SARFAESI Act on various systems, etc. have been discussed.

It is hoped that this book will be helpful to bank officials who are dealing with the SARFAESI proceedings, lawyers, students and various customers of the Banks.

The author is grateful to the bank officials, judicial officers and the advocates who have given valuable suggestions and feedback in the preparation of this book.

The author will be glad to receive suggestions for further improvements to this book. Wishing a wonderful reading experience to all.

Dr. Syamjith Parakkott

Acknowledgements

My acknowledgment to the State Bank of India, my esteemed organisation, for the support, guidance and opportunity to learn and gain expertise in writing this book.

Chapter 1

An exploration of the SARFAESI Act – practical insights

Introduction

As the name suggests, this book, entitled *An Exploration of the SARFAESI ACT – Practical Insights*, is an exploration into the various provisions of the SARFAESI Act, its practical insights and its implications on various systems. Like any other enactment passed by Parliament, the SARFAESI Act has both positive and negative implications. While the enactment of the SARFAESI Act was necessary to curb the growing menace of non-performing assets (hereinafter referred to as NPAs), it has also resulted in violations of the rights of borrowers and guarantors. The bankers in India insisted on such a legislation as they need the enactment to create a level playing field with their foreign counter parts. The SARFAESI Act has enabled Indian bankers to take possession of the property without going through the long drawn court proceedings as in other developed countries. This book describes the evolution and development of recovery laws relating to banks and financial institutions. In this book, the jurisprudence of debt recovery laws has been analysed in detail. This book also highlights the issues and challenges in enforcing the SARFAESI Act and its implications on various systems. The book also describes how the Insolvency and Bankruptcy Code has become a big game changer for Indian banking.

Money is the driving force behind all enterprises. It is the fountainhead of trade and commerce. When sufficient money is not available in the economy, it is not possible to promote any trade and commerce. A short-term or long-term assistance of financing to promote business is the need of the day. The banks in India provide short-term, long-term, and mini-term financial assistance for the growth of agricultural and industrial activities in the country. As a result of rapid growth in the industrial area, the role of the banks has become very dynamic in achieving the highest levels of industrialisation and developments in agriculture.

The Section 5 (b) of the Banking Regulation Act defines banking as the acceptance of deposits of money from the public for the purpose of lending

DOI: 10.4324/9781003546238-1

or investment. Such deposits may be repayable on demand or otherwise and withdrawable by cheque, draft, order or otherwise. In essence, a banker is collecting money from the public and lending it to needy persons in society. The banker will be in trouble if the persons who received the money don't repay in a timely manner. So, lending and recovery are two sides of a coin for a banker. The success of a banking business depends largely on keeping the equilibrium between the deposits and advances. The default amount that the banker suffers is called non-performing assets. The upward swing in the level of default results in the weakening ability of a banker to lend money to needy people.

Before the Recovery of Debts Due to Banks and Financial Institutions Act, 1993, was placed in the statute book, banks had to institute a suit in a court with civil jurisdiction for the recovery of debts due to banks and financial institutions. The way in which they had to recover the debts always had inordinate delays in the settlement of their claims because civil courts are flooded with cases for adjudication. A significant portion of the funds of banks and financial institutions were thus blocked in unproductive assets, the value of which kept deteriorating with the passage of time. The borrowers and guarantors were also facing difficulties due to the delay in delivery of justice.

The legal procedures in existence prior to 1993 for the recovery of debts due to banks and financial institutions were time consuming and ineffective and had blocked a significant portion of the funds in unproductive assets. In 1981, a committee under the chairmanship of Shri. T. Tiwari examined the legal and other difficulties faced by banks and suggested remedial measures including changes in the law. The Tiwari Committee also suggested setting up special tribunals for the recovery of dues to banks and financial institutions by following a summary procedure.

In 1991, the Committee on the Financial System, constituted by the Central Government under the chairmanship of Shri. M. Narasimham, recommended that the government should set up special tribunals to expedite the recovery process. Accordingly, Parliament enacted the Recovery of Debts Due to Banks and Financial Institutions Act, 1993, with the objective of providing for expeditious adjudication and the recovery of debts due to banks and financial institutions through the Debt Recovery Tribunal. The Act came into force on 24th June 1993 and intended to provide for expeditious adjudication and recovery of debts due to banks and financial institutions.

With the advent of the Recovery of Debts Due to Banks and Financial Institutions Act, 1993 (This Act was renamed as The Recovery of Debts and Bankruptcy Act vide Act 31 of 2016 and hereinafter referred to as DRT Act), it was expected that most of the non-performing assets would be easy to recover from defaulters. However, it was realised in due course that the enactment of the DRT Act was not enough to fight the menace of NPAs and deliver justice to the genuine borrowers/guarantors. With the objective of giving more powers and skills to banks and delivering justice to the affected parties, the government decided to bring in the SARFAESI Act.

During this period, there was pressure on the banks to achieve international standards, and the banks in India were progressively complying with the international prudential norms and standards. The banks in India demanded a level playing field with international banks. Prior to 2002, there was no provision for facilitating securitisation of financial assets or to take possession of securitised assets and sell them off.

The SARFAESI Act was enacted with the intention to strengthen the creditors' rights through enforcement of securities by banks and financial institutions by conferring on the creditors the right to seize and sell the secured assets in order to recover the dues promptly and bypass the costly and time-consuming legal court process.

The legal framework in existence prior to the enactment of the SARFAESI Act had not kept pace with the changing commercial practices and financial sector reforms. The old legal framework resulted in a slow pace of recovery of defaulting loans and the mounting levels of non-performing assets of banks of and financial institutions. The Narasimham Committee II and Andhyarujina Committee constituted by the Central Government for the purpose of examining banking sector reforms considered the need for changes in the legal system in respect to these areas. These committees, *inter alia*, suggested the enactment of a new legislation for securitisation and to empower banks and financial institutions to take possession and sell the securities without the intervention of the court. Acting on these suggestions, the Securitisation and Reconstruction of Financial Assets and Enforcement of Security Interest Ordinance, 2002, was promulgated by the Central Government on 21st June 2002 to regulate the securitisation and reconstruction of financial assets and the enforcement of security interest and for matters connected therewith and incidental thereto. The ordinance received the assent of the president and became an act on 18th December 2002.

The SARFAESI Act was enacted to enable banks to realise long-term assets, manage the problem of liquidity and asset liability mismatches and improve recovery by exercising powers to take possession and sell securities and to reduce non-performing assets by adopting the measures as stipulated under the provisions of SARFAESI Act.

The SARFAESI Act basically deals with four aspects:

- Enforcement of security interest by secured creditors/banks.
- Transfer of non-performing assets to an asset reconstruction company.
- Provide a legal framework for the securitisation of assets.
- Provide for adjudication of grievances of the affected persons.

The constitutional validity of the SARFAESI Act came under the consideration of the Hon'ble Supreme Court of India in the popular case of *Mardia Chemicals Ltd v. Union of India.*[1] The Hon'ble Supreme Court of India upheld the validity of the Act and its provisions except that of Sub-Section (2) of Section 17 of the Act, which was declared *ultra vires* of Article 14 of the Constitution of India. It was also observed that where a secured creditor has taken action under Section 13(4) of the Act, the borrowers/guarantors would be allowed to file appeals under Section 17 of the Act, within the limitation period.

Thereafter, although the SARFAESI Act enabled bankers to recover a good amount of money, due to multiple reasons such as litigations, inordinate delays in the disposal of applications/appeals, bottlenecks in taking physical possession of the secured assets, etc., the bankers found it difficult to enforce the provisions of the Act in its full effect. The result is that the recovery expected by enforcing the SARFAESI falls short of expectations.

Thereafter, the government focussed its attention on insolvency and bankruptcy laws. The government decided to consolidate the laws relating to insolvency and bankruptcy in India with the objective of allowing credit to flow more freely in India and instilling faith in investors for speedy disposals of their claims. The insolvency resolution process in India has in the past involved the simultaneous operation of several statutory instruments. These include the Presidency Towns Insolvency Act, 1909; Provincial Insolvency Act, 1920; Sick Industrial Companies Act, 1985;

Securitisation and Reconstruction of Financial Assets and Enforcement of Security Interest Act, 2002; Recovery of Debt Due to Banks and Financial Institutions Act, 1993; and Companies Act, 2013. Broadly, these statutes provided for a disparate process of debt restructuring and asset seizure and the ability to facilitate the satisfaction of outstanding debts. The multiple legal avenues and a hamstrung court system in India witnessed a huge pile up of non-performing assets and creditors waiting for years to recover their money. The Parliament introduced the Insolvency and Bankruptcy Code (hereinafter referred to as IBC), 2016, which was considered as the most powerful weapon to reduce the frightening level of non-performance assets. It was expected that the IBC would change the game plan of NPA management in the Indian banking space. The Code consolidates existing laws relating to insolvency of corporate entities and individuals into a single legislation. The Code has unified the laws relating to enforcement of the statutory rights of creditors and streamlined the way a debtor company can be revived to sustain its debt without extinguishing the rights of creditors.

The main objectives of the code are time-bound reorganisation, maximisation of the value of assets, promotion of entrepreneurship, availability of credit and the balanced interests of all stakeholders. The first-order objective is resolution. The second-order objective is maximisation of the value of the assets of the firm, and the third-order objective is promoting entrepreneurship, availability of credit and balancing the interests of various stake holders.

* * * * * * * * * * * * * *

Note

1 Mardia Chemicals Ltd v. Union of India, AIR 2004 SC 2371.

Chapter 2

The evolution and development of recovery laws relating to banks and financial institutions

The term "banking" always revolves around the concept of 'lending money' and facilitating the growth of various sectors of the economy. The lending of money enables banking institutions to earn profit for their survival. The credit options extended by banks generally take the following three forms:[1]

(1) Cash credit
(2) Overdrafts
(3) Loans.

Let's discuss cash credit first. In simple banking parlance, a "cash credit" is an arrangement by a bank made with its customer to borrow money up to a certain limit against the values of his stocks and book debts for his day-to-day requirements. The various borrowers, such as companies, partnership firms or proprietorship firms, use the cash credit from banks to meet their day-to-day financial requirements.

The term "overdraft" is a temporary accommodation that allows a customer to overdraw his current account, usually against collateral securities. The borrowers generally use an overdraft to meet urgent financial requirements.

The term "loans" generally means advances made by a banker in a lump sum, the whole of which is withdrawn and is supposed to be repaid, generally wholly, at any time or by way of equated monthly instalments during the fixed period. The loans that are payable on demand from the bank are called demand loans, and the loans that are payable by way of equated monthly instalments are called term loans.

The banks extend credit facilities to borrowers under the agreement that the money received will be repaid as per the schedule. On repayment, the money received shall be circulated among the public who are in need of financial support. However, when the money granted by the banks fails to return, the banks face a situation of out of funds. This will result in the failure to

DOI: 10.4324/9781003546238-2

extend the credit facilities to needy persons in society, ultimately resulting in adverse impact on the economy. This vicious circle has got far reaching consequences and the health of the country's economy will also be at stake. While analysing the rights of bankers *vis-à-vis* the duty cast upon the borrowers to repay the dues, it is to be noted that the bankers' right to recover their dues are of paramount importance. However, it must be ensured that the bankers' right to recovery of dues from the borrowers/guarantors is strictly guided by the provisions of the applicable laws. The recovery of money from defaulted borrowers through various legal recourses is a matter of large importance for banks. However, it is equally important that the legal measures exercised by banks confirm to the principles of natural justice and are not in violation of the rights guaranteed to the borrowers/guarantors under the various provisions of the laws in force.

In banking parlance, the concept of "recovery of dues" from the borrowers/guarantors has two stages (Figure 2.1).

The first stage is "soft recovery", wherein the bankers adopt soft techniques for the recovery of dues such as issuing letters to borrowers, meeting them in person, visiting their residence, place of business or office, etc. In this stage, the bankers are not adopting the strict enforcement of legal provisions but are pursuing the borrowers/guarantors to repay their dues without resorting to legal proceedings. In the second stage, the bankers are resorting to the enforcement of legal proceedings before the appropriate judicial forum for adjudication of their dues.

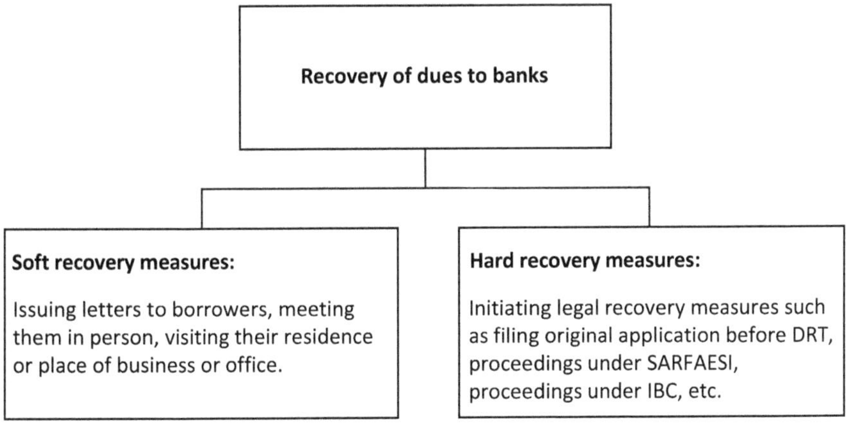

Figure 2.1 Stages of the concept of recovery of dues

I. Different stages of evolution of recovery laws

It is interesting to understand how the recovery laws pertaining to banking have evolved and developed over time. We can divide the evolution and development of the recovery laws relating to banking institutions into four stages. They are as follows:

- The period up to the enactment of The Recovery of Debts Due to Banks and Financial Institutions Act, 1993, is called as the *Pre-DRT stage.*
- The period from the enactment of The Recovery of Debts Due to Banks and Financial Institutions Act, 1993, up to the enactment of the Securitisation and Reconstruction of Financial Assets and Enforcement of Security Interest Act, 2002, is called the *DRT stage.*
- The period from the enactment of the Securitisation and Reconstruction of Financial Assets and Enforcement of Security Interest Act, 2002, and thereafter is called the *SARFAESI stage.*
- The period from the enactment of the Insolvency and Bankruptcy Code, 2016, and thereafter is called the *IBC stage.*

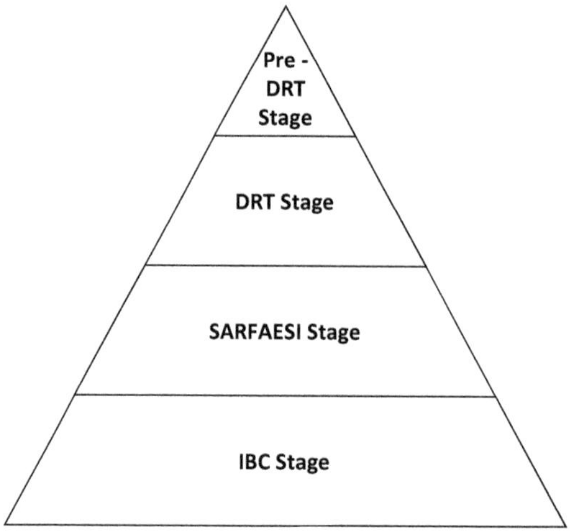

Figure 2.2 Pyramid chart – the evolution of banking recovery laws through various stages

The evolution of banking recovery laws through various stages can be better explained with the help of the pyramid chart in Figure 2.2.

During the first stage, the Pre-DRT stage, the banks resorted to the provisions of the Civil Procedure Code, 1908, to file suit against the borrowers/guarantors who defaulted in repaying their dues. The bankers instituted the plaint by invoking the provisions of the Civil Procedure Code under Order VII, Section 26 and other relevant provisions. After the institution of the plaint, the concerned courts adjudicated the claim of the bank after issuing notice to the defendants and on the verification of all relevant documents and arguments of both parties.

Most of the loans and advances granted by banks are generally secured by the tangible security of valuable collateral such as bonds, shares, merchandise in the godowns, motor vehicles under hypothecation and mortgages of immovable property. However, loans such as personal loans, educational loans, etc. are granted on personal liability and without any tangible security.

In loan accounts, where collateral security is available, the banks are at liberty to file suits to enforce the securities. However, with accounts where there is no collateral security, the banks may need to file suits against borrowers on personal liability and obtain a personal decree and enforce the same by filing execution petitions. In loan accounts, where the borrower created a mortgage in favour of the bank as security for the money advanced to him, the banks can file a mortgage suit to enforce the mortgage rights.

In the Pre-DRT stage, i.e. period up to the enactment of the Recovery of Debts Due to Banks and Financial Institutions Act, 1993, the bankers were required to file all suits for recovery of money before the concerned courts with civil jurisdiction. Since the civil courts were burdened with a large number of cases, the suits filed by banks were delayed and bankers received decrees after waiting for a considerable period, say 3 to 5 years. Due to the long delays in getting a decree, instances of security being diluted and the disposal of security by the borrowers became very common. Further, the usual procedures adopted in civil courts also contributed to the delay of awarding decrees in cases filed by banks.

In this context, the Committee on the Financial System convened by the Government of India under the chairmanship of Shri. M. Narasimham in August 1991 examined the feasibility of setting up special tribunals for the adjudication of recovery cases of banks with special powers for adjudication and speedy recoveries. As per the data on 30th September 1990, more than 15 lakhs of cases filed by public sector banks and about 304 cases filed by financial institutions were pending in various courts and more than Rs.5622 crores in dues of public sector banks and about Rs.391 crores in dues of the financial institutions were involved in these cases. Locking up such a huge amount of public money in litigation prevented the proper utilisation and recycling of the funds for the development of the country.

The account/asset that turned into bad debt due to non-payment of principal or interest in banking terminology is non-performing assets (hereinafter referred to as NPAs). In terms of the notification[2] issued by the Reserve Bank of India on prudent norms on income recognition, asset classification and provisioning pertaining to advances, an asset, including a leased asset, becomes non-performing when it ceases to generate income for the bank. An amount is considered to be overdue if it is not paid on the due date fixed by the bank. The increase in the level of NPAs beyond a certain level is a cause for concern for all stakeholders in the financial sector because the availability of credit is essential for the economic growth of the country and the accumulation of NPAs affect the smooth flow of credit. Although there may be genuine reasons for the borrowers/guarantors to repay the dues, the rights of the banks to recovery dues from defaulted borrowers/guarantors can't be ignored based on those grounds. It is important to note that the Indian banks, as per the instructions from the Reserve Bank of India, have come up with the One Time Settlement and other compromise schemes to support the genuine borrowers. The genuine borrowers should make sincere attempts to settle their dues under the One Time Settlement or other compromise schemes. The banks raise resources not just on fresh deposits, but also by recycling the funds received from the borrowers. Thus, when a loan becomes non-performing, it affects the entire recycling of credit and credit creation.[3]

It is a fact that the financial sector plays a pivotal role in India's efforts to achieve success in progressively developing its economy. During the 1980s, the banking sector in India was making efforts to comply with the international prudential norms and accounting practices. But there were certain areas in which the Indian banking and financial sector did not have a level playing field with other participants in financial markets in the world. The major concerns by the Indian banking industry during this period were a lack of legal provisions to facilitate the securitisation of financial assets of banks and financial institutions and the direct enforcement of securities without going through the cumbersome legal process.

Under such circumstances, the Tiwari Committee, in its report,[4] held that in respect of suits by banks and financial institutions, there had been abnormal delays in various courts at the trial stage as well as at the execution stage, and hence it stated that

> the principle that the State should have a special procedure to enforce its own demands should equally be extended to the recovery of dues of banks and financial institutions as well.

The recommendation of the Tiwari Committee made the following points:

(1) The committee emphasised the constitution of the Tribunal should have the same principle as that of a state; where a state has a special procedure to enforce its own demands, the bankers should have a Special Tribunal to enforce its dues.
(2) The committee recommended that a tribunal under Arts. 323-A and 323-B of the constitution should be constituted.

(3) The committee further recommended that the Tribunal should not be bogged down by the Code of Civil Procedure, 1908, but it should have a simple procedure guided only by principles of natural justice.

1. The evolution of the recovery laws – Pre-DRT stage

In the Pre-DRT stage, the banks were filing suits before the competent courts under Section 26 and Order VII Rule I of the Code of Civil Procedure for the recovery of the dues. These suits were adjudicated by the civil courts along with other cases. Since the suits filed by banks didn't receive any preferences, it took years to get a decree. Further, the execution petition filed in pursuance of the decree also took its own time to complete the process. Since the banks are involved in the distribution of public money for the development of the social and economic features of the country, the blocking of large amount of money in lengthy litigation has adversely affected the interest of the country. Under these circumstances, the banking industry demanded a separate tribunal for the adjudication of their claims.

The statement of objectives and reasons[5] of the Recovery of Debts Due to Banks and Financial Institutions Act, 1993, reflect the concern of the Indian Parliament towards the difficulties faced by banks and financial institutions in recovering loans and the enforcement of securities charged with them. The Parliament, in the statement of objectives of the Act, admitted that the existing procedure for the recovery of debts due to the banks and financial institutions blocked a significant portion of their funds in unproductive assets, the value of which deteriorates with the passage of time.

2. Enactment of the Recovery of Debts Due to Banks and Financial Institutions Act, 1993 – DRT stage

The Recovery of Debts Due to Banks and Financial Institutions Act, 1993 (DRT Act) was enacted to facilitate for the creation of specialised forums, i.e. the Debts Recovery Tribunals and the Debts Recovery Appellate Tribunals, for expeditious adjudication of disputes relating to recovery of the debts due to banks and financial institutions. Simultaneously, the jurisdiction of the civil courts was barred and all pending matters were transferred to the Tribunals from the date of their establishment.

The DRT Act provided for the establishment of the tribunals and the appellate tribunals with the jurisdiction, powers and authority to make summary adjudication of applications made by banks or financial institutions. It also specified the modes of recovery of the amount determined by the tribunal or the appellate tribunal. The DRT Act also barred the jurisdiction of all courts except the Supreme Court and the High Courts in relation to the matters specified in Section 17. The Tribunals and the Appellate Tribunals have also been freed from the shackles of procedure contained in the Code of Civil Procedure. To put it differently, the DRT Act not only brought into existence the special procedural mechanism for a speedy recovery of the dues of banks and financial institutions, but it also made provisions for ensuring that defaulting borrowers were not able to invoke the jurisdiction of civil courts for frustrating the proceedings initiated by the banks and other financial institutions.

At the initial stage, the tribunals faced problems in functioning effectively. However, after the judgement of the Hon'ble Supreme Court, which upheld the constitutional validity of the DRT Act in the case of *Union of India v. Delhi High Court Bar Association*,[6] the Tribunals were fully functional. The Union government also took steps to fill the gaps in the DRT Act by enacting a further amendment to the Act. As a consequence to the establishment of tribunals, the cases pending before the civil courts above Rs.10 lakhs and decreed cases above Rs.10 lakhs were transferred to the DRTs.

Though the initial progress of Debt Recovery Tribunals were impressive, subsequently the tribunals faced the fate of other Courts/Tribunals. An analysis of the amount recovered through the DRT revealed that the entire process of recovery of overdue loans through DRTs didn't show much progress, despite the functioning of the full-fledged Debt Recovery Tribunals. One of the reasons for such slow progress in recovery was the procedural delay in the DRT in disposing cases and the lack of required powers and skills on the part of the banks/financial institutions to enforce the securities without approaching the courts.

3. *The enactment of the Securitisation and Reconsturction of Financial Assets and Enforcement of Security Interest Act, 2002 – SARFAESI stage*

Acting on the suggestions of the Narasimham Committees I and II and the Andhyarujna Committee, the Securitisation and Reconstruction of Financial Assets and Enforcement of Security Interest Act, 2002, was promulgated by the Central Government on 21st June 2002 to regulate securitisation and the reconstruction of financial assets and the enforcement of security interest and for matters connected therewith or incidental thereto. The Act, in effect, enabled the banks and financial institutions to realise long-term assets, manage the problems of liquidity and asset liability mismatches and improve recovery by exercising powers to take possession and sell securities and reduce non-performing assets by adopting measures for recovery or reconstruction.

The enactment of the Securitisation and Reconsturction of Financial Assets and Enforcement of Security Interest Act, 2002 (the SARFAESI Act) was one of the most radical legislative measures taken by Parliament to ensure that dues of secured creditors, including banks and financial institutions, were recovered from the defaulting borrowers without any obstruction. For the first time, the secured creditors were empowered to take steps for recovery of their dues without the intervention of the courts or tribunals. However, effective implementation of the SARFAESI Act was delayed by more than 2 years because several writ petitions filed in the High Courts and the Supreme Court questioning the vires of the Act. The matter was finally decided by the Hon'ble Supreme Court in *Mardia Chemicals v. Union of India*,[7] and the validity of the SARFAESI Act was upheld, except for the condition of the deposit of a 75% amount enshrined in Section 17(2). While writing the judgement, the Supreme Court referred to the recommendations of the Narasimham and Andhyarujina Committees on the issue of the constitution of special tribunals to deal with cases relating to the recovery of the dues of banks, etc. and observed that one of the measures recommended was to vest the financial institutions through special statues and the power of sale of the assets without intervention of the court and for reconstruction of assets.

The Hon'ble Supreme Court observed that the question of non-recoverable or delayed recovery of debts advanced by the banks was considered in-depth by the committees. In some situations, where the amounts of dues are huge and a hope of early recovery is small, it cannot be said that a more effective legislation for the purpose was uncalled for or that it could not be resorted to. It is again to be noted that after the report of the Narasimham Committee, yet another committee was constituted, headed by Mr. Andhyarujina, to bring about the needed steps within the legal framework. While upholding the constitutionality of the SARFAESI Act, the Hon'ble Supreme Court was unable to find much substance in the submission made on behalf of the petitioners that while the Recovery of Debts Due to Banks and Financial Institutions Act was in operation it was uncalled for to have yet another legislation like the SARFAESI Act for the recovery of the mounting dues. Considering the totality of circumstances and the financial climate worldwide, if it was a matter of policy to have a speedier legal method to recover the dues, such a policy decision could not be faulted nor was it a matter to be sent to the courts to test the legitimacy of such a measure relating to financial policy.

On examination of various judgements of Supreme Court on the SARFAESI Act, it can be observed that the spirit and intention of the Parliament in enacting the SARFAESI Act was upheld by the Hon'ble Supreme Court of India. A typical example is the judgement in *United Bank of India v. Satyawat Tondon and Others*,[8] wherein the Hon'ble Supreme Court observed that many hundreds of thousands took advantage of easy financing by the banks and other financial institutions, but a large number of them did not repay the amount of the loan. Additionally, they instituted frivolous cases and succeeded in persuading the civil courts to pass orders of injunction against the steps taken by banks and financial institutions to recover their dues. Due to lack of adequate infrastructure and non-availability of manpower, the regular courts could not accomplish the task of expeditiously adjudicating the cases instituted by banks and other financial institutions for recovery of their dues. As a result, the Supreme Court noted that several hundred crores of public money were blocked in unproductive ventures.

4. *The evolution of the recovery laws – IBC stage*

Although the SARFAESI Act enabled bankers to recover good amount of money, multiple litigations, inordinate delays in the disposal of applications/appeals, bottlenecks in taking physical possession of the secured assets, etc. made it difficult for bankers to enforce the provisions of the Act in full effect. This has prompted the government to consolidate laws relating to insolvency and bankruptcy in India with an objective to allow credit to flow more freely in India and to instill faith in investors for a speedy disposal of their claims. The insolvency resolution process in India has in the past involved the simultaneous operation of several statutory instruments. These include the Presidency Towns Insolvency Act, 1909; Provincial Insolvency Act, 1920; Sick Industrial Companies Act, 1985; Securitisation and Reconstruction of Financial Assets and Enforcement of Security Interest Act, 2002; Recovery of Debt Due to Banks and Financial Institutions Act, 1993; and Companies Act, 2013. Broadly, these statutes provided for a disparate process of debt restructuring and asset seizure and realisation in order to facilitate the satisfaction of outstanding debts. The multiple legal avenues and multiple layers of the court system in India witnessed a huge pile up of non-performing assets and creditors waiting for years to recover their money. The IBC consolidated existing laws relating to the insolvency of corporate entities and individuals into a single legislation. The IBC unified the law relating to the enforcement of statutory rights of creditors and streamlined the manner in which a debtor company can be revived to sustain its debt without extinguishing the rights of creditors.

It is important to note that the government and regulators such as RBI had been working on various measures to improve the enforcement of the provisions of the recovery laws. The Reserve Bank, on 30th January 2014, issued a "Framework to Revitalise the Distressed Assets in the Economy", wherein banks would recognise at an early stage the stress in their assets and take prompt steps towards resolution/recovery of distressed assets. The framework identified certain structural impediments in the way of a smooth resolution/recovery of stressed assets of banks and also suggested steps, such as revamping the SARFAESI Act, revitalising DRTs, rejuvenating asset reconstruction companies, etc.[9]

* * * * * * * * * * * * * * *

Notes

1 *Tannan's Banking*; M L TANNAN – Twenty Third Edition-Lexis Nexis.
2 RBI notification on prudential norms on income recognition, asset classification and provision pertaining to advances dated 1 April 2022.
3 Banking sector reforms and NPA: A study of Indian Commercial Banks-working paper by Meenakshi Rajeev and H P Mahesh- Institute for Social and Economic Change, Bangalore.

4 Tiwari Committee report of 1981, Chapter VIII, para. 8.23.
5 Statement of objectives and reasons of the Recovery of Debts due to Banks and Financial Institutions Act, 1993 (Act No. 51 of 1993).
6 Union of India v. Delhi High Court Bar Association, AIR 2002 SC 1479.
7 Mardia Chemicals v. Union of India, 2004(4) SCC 311.
8 United Bank of India v. Satyawati Tondon and Others arising out of SLP© No.10145 of 2010.
9 "Banks in India: Challenges & Opportunities" – Keynote address delivered by Shri Harun R Khan, Deputy Governor at the BFSI Conference 2014 organized by SBICap Securities on 12 June 2014 in Mumbai.

Chapter 3

The constitutional and regulatory frameworks of recovery laws relating to banks and financial institutions

It is generally believed that the processes involved in a suit filed for recovery of debts before a civil court are disconcerting to the banks/financial institutions. More often, protracted delay in recovering debt result in loss to the banks/financial institutions in real terms, as the time spent for the process itself would have caused substantially loss to the bank in terms of manpower and resources, even if recovered fully. The delay in litigation would have equally affected the parties on the other side also, i.e. the borrowers and guarantors, by exposing them to costly and time-consuming legal battles. Therefore, in order to provide the banks and financial institutions with more efficient mode of recovery of debts, the Legislature provided for the establishment of special courts by enacting the Recovery of Debts Due to Banks and Financial Institutions Act, 1993.

I. The constitutionality of the provisions of the Recovery of Debts Due to Banks and Financial Institutions Act, 1993

Several writ petitions were filed in different High Courts in India challenging the constitutionality of the DRT Act. On analysis of the judgements of various High Courts, the legal issues highlighted by different High Courts are summarised in the following sections.

1. *The Delhi High Court Judgement*

The validity of the DRT Act was first challenged before the Delhi High Court. By its decision in *Delhi High Court Bar Association and Another v. Union of India and Others*,[1] the Delhi High Court held that although a tribunal could be constituted by Parliament – even though it was not within the purview of Arts.323-A and 323-B of the Constitution and that the expression "administration of justice" as appearing in Entry 11-A of List III of the Seventh Schedule to the Constitution would include tribunals as well administering

DOI: 10.4324/9781003546238-3

justice – the DRT Act was unconstitutional because it eroded the independence of the judiciary and was irrational, discriminatory, unreasonable and arbitrary, and it was struck by Art. 14 of the Constitution.

The reasoning given by the High Court when declaring the Recovery of Debts Due to Banks and Financial Institutions Act, 1993, as irrational and arbitrary was that Section 17 of the Act did not have a provision for a counterclaim as provided under the provisions of the Code of Civil Procedure. The Act also lowered the authority of the High Court *vis-à-vis* the Tribunal because suits for recovery of money exceeding Rs.10 lakhs were to be filed before the Tribunal, while the suits for an amount between Rs.5 lakhs and Rs.10 lakhs were to be filed before the Delhi High Court and for less than Rs.5 lakhs before the subordinate courts. This lowered the status of the High Court in as much as the Tribunal, which was presided by an officer who did not have the status of a High Court Judge, would be deciding the suits for recovery of money exceeding Rs.10 lakhs.

Another criticism against the Act was that it eroded the independence of the judiciary since the jurisdiction of civil courts had been truncated and vested in the Tribunal. It also came to the conclusion that the independence of the judiciary was eroded as the High Court had no role to play in the appointment of the presiding officers.

2. *The Gauhati High Court Judgement*

The Gauhati High Court also considered the validity of the DRT Act. By judgement in *Assam Leather Industry v. Union of India (UOI) and Others*,[2] the High Court came to the conclusion that although the Parliament had the legislative competence to enact the law, it had abrogated/negated the power of judicial review, and the Act was void as it had violated the basic features of the Constitution. It further held that Section 17 needed to be stuck down because it gave jurisdiction, powers and authority that were unreasonable. It also struck down the appointment of a recovery officer and held that the modes for recovery of debts under Section 25 and 28(1) and (2) were arbitrary, unreasonable and without any guidelines, control, etc. It further quashed Section 31, which dealt with the transfer of suits/proceedings, and Section 34(1), which gave overriding effect to the Act.

3. *Karnataka High Court Judgement*

While considering the validity of the DRT Act, the Karnataka High Court, in the case of *D.K. Abdul Khader and Others v. Union of India and Others*,[3] came to the conclusion that the Parliament did not have the legislative competence to enact the Act in as much as Entry 11-A of List III could not include a "Tribunal", and furthermore the Parliament could not exercise power to enact this law under the provisions of Arts. 323-A or 323-B of the Constitution. In other words, a tribunal could not be constituted for any matter not specified in Arts. 323-A or 323-B.

4. *The Supreme Court of India Judgement*

All the aforesaid decisions of the High Court were challenged before the Hon'ble Supreme Court of *India in Union of India and Another v. Delhi High Court Bar Association and Others.*[4] The main contentions of the critics of the DRT Act were that the Act was unreasonable and are violated Art. 14 of the Constitution and that the same is beyond the legislative competence of the Parliament. The Hon'ble Supreme Court, while analysing the orders of the High Court, made the following observations:

(i) The Supreme Court held that the power of Parliament to enact a law, which is not covered by an Entry, List II and List III, is absolute.

(ii) While Arts. 323-A and 323-B specifically enable the legislatures to enact laws for the establishment of Tribunals, in relation to the matters specified therein, the power of the Parliament to enact a law constituting a Tribunal, like the Banking Tribunal, which is not covered by any of the matters specified in Art 323-A or 323-B, is not taken away.

(iii) Articles 323-A and 323-B are enabling provisions which specifically enable the setting up of Tribunals contemplated by the said Articles. These Articles, however, cannot be interpreted to mean that it prohibits the legislature from establishing Tribunals not covered by these Articles, as long as there is legislative competence under an appropriate entry in the Seventh Schedule. Articles 323-A and 323-B do not take away that legislative competence. The contrary view expressed by the Karnataka High Court in D.K. Abdul Khader's case[5] does not lay down the correct law and the Ld. Supreme Court expressly disapproves of the same.

(iv) The Supreme Court held that the Entry 45 of List I relate to "Banking". The banking operations would, *inter alia*, include accepting of loans and deposits, granting of loans and recovery of the debts due to the bank. The recovery of dues is an essential function of any banking institution. In exercise of its legislative power relating to banking, the parliament can provide the mechanism by which monies due to the Banks and Financial Institutions can be recovered. The tribunals have been set up in regard to the debts due to the banks. The special machinery of a tribunal which has been constituted as per the preamble of the Act "for expeditious adjudication and recovery of debts due to banks and financial institutions and for matters connected therewith or incidental thereto" would squarely fall within the ambit of Entry 45 of List I. Setting up of an adjudicatory body like the Banking Tribunal relating to transactions in which banks and financial institutions are concerned would clearly fall under Entry 45 of List I giving the Parliament specific power to legislate in relation thereto.

(v) The Supreme Court didn't agree with the decision of the Delhi High Court that the DRT Act or any other provision thereof is in any way arbitrary or bad in law. During the pendency of these appeals, the DRT Act has been amended and whatever lacunae or infirmities existed have now been removed by the said Amending Act and with the framing of more rules. For example: Rules have been framed in 1998 for the appointing of Presiding Officers of the Tribunals as well as the Presiding Officers of the Appellate Tribunals. The Rules contemplate appointments being made by a Selection Committee. Each of the Selection Committee is to consist of the Chief Justice of India or a Judge of the Supreme Court as nominated by the Chief Justice of India along with other members referred to in the said Rules. The Selection Committee so constituted would ensure fair and impartial selection of competent persons to act as Presiding Officers of the Tribunal.

(vi) The Supreme Court held that there is no absolute right in anyone to demand that his dispute is to be adjudicated upon only by a Civil Court. It is by reason of the provisions of the Code of Civil Procedure that the Civil Courts had the right, prior to the enactment of the Debt Recovery Act, to decide the suits for recovery filed by the banks and financial institutions. This forum, namely, that of a Civil Court, now stands replaced by a Banking Tribunal in respect of the debts due to the bank. When in the Constitution Arts.323-A and 323-B contemplate establishment of a Tribunal and that does not erode the independence of the judiciary, there is no reason to presume that the Banking Tribunals and the Appellate Tribunals so constituted would not be independent or that justice would be denied to the defendants or that the independence of the judiciary would stand eroded.

(vii) The Supreme Court held that the Tribunals, whether they pertain to Income-tax or Sales Tax or Excise and Customs or Administration, have now become an essential part of the judicial system in this country. Such specialized institutions may not strictly come within the concept of the judiciary, as envisaged by Art.50, but it cannot be presumed that such Tribunals are not an effective part of the justice delivery system, like Courts of law. It will be seen that for a person to be appointed as a Presiding Officer of DRT, he should be one who is qualified to be a District Judge and in case of appointment of the Presiding Officer of the appellate Tribunal he is or has been, qualified to be a judge of a High Court or has been a member of the Indian Legal Service who has held a post in Grade I for at least three years. The Supreme Court further held that it has to be borne in mind that the decision of the appellate Tribunal is not final, in the sense that the same can be subjected to judicial review by the High Court under Arts.226 and 227 of the Constitution.

(viii) The Supreme Court held that with the establishment of the Tribunals, Section 31 provides for the transfer of pending cases from Civil Courts to the Tribunal. The Supreme Court does not find such a provision being in any way bad in law. Once a Debt Recovery Tribunal has been established and the jurisdiction of Courts barred by Section 18 of the Act, it would be only logical that any matter pending in the Civil Court should stand transferred to the Tribunal.

(ix) The Supreme Court held that ". . . Guwahati High Court held that Sections 25 and 28 are arbitrary and unreasonable, being without any guidelines or control. These observations were made prior to the amendment of Sections 25 and 28. After amendment, Section 25 provides for modes of recovery of debts either by attachment and sale or arrest or appointment of a Receiver and Section 28 provides for modes of recovery in addition to the ones specified in Section 25". The Hon'ble Supreme Court held that a perusal of the aforesaid provisions cannot lead one to the conclusion that the same are arbitrary, unreasonable or without any guidelines. The Supreme Court further added that it is quite clear that in order to recover the debts, the Recovery Officer has to attach and sell the immovable property and that for protection and preservation of the same, he has the power to appoint a Receiver for the management thereof.

(x) The Supreme Court held that "By virtue of Section 29 of the Act, the provisions of the Second and Third Schedules to the Income-tax Act, 1961 and the Income Tax (Certificate Proceedings) Rules, 1962, has become applicable for the realization of the dues by the Recovery Officer. Detailed procedure for recovery is contained in these schedules to the Income-tax Act, including provisions relating to arrest and detention of the defaulter. It cannot, therefore, be said that the Recovery Officer would act in an arbitrary manner. Furthermore, Section 30, after amendment by the Amendment Act, 2000, gives a right to any person aggrieved by an order of the Recovery Officer, to prefer an appeal to the Tribunal. There is, therefore, sufficient safeguard which has been provided in the event of the Recovery Officer acting in an arbitrary or unreasonable manner. The provisions of Sections 25 and 28 are, therefore, not bad in law".

(xi) The Hon'ble Court while allowing the appeals of the Union of India and the Bank held that the Recovery of Debts Due to Banks and Financial Institutions Act, 1993 is a valid piece of legislation. As a result, thereof, the writ petitions or appeals filed by various parties challenging the validity of the said Act or some of the provisions thereof are dismissed.

After declaring the DRT Act constitutionally valid by the Hon'ble Supreme Court, the Tribunals, as constituted under the Act, became functional and started delivering judgements. The main point of difference between a proceeding before the Tribunal and a suit before a civil court is, firstly, in the procedures required to be followed by each; secondly, in the need of the applicant to establish the existence of debt; and thirdly, in the scope for hearing arguments over technical lapses of the creditor, if any. The proceedings before the Debt Recovery Tribunals are guided by the principles of natural justice and the burden to prove that the debt is not in existence is on the borrower/guarantor. It is the obligation of the borrower/guarantor to point out the technical lapses of the creditor before the Tribunal. It is fact that since the proceedings before the Tribunal are guided by the principle of natural justice and not by the rules under Civil Procedure Code, the proceedings were faster than the civil courts.

As the Recovery of Debts Due to Banks and Financial Institutions Act, 1993, was made in haste, there were certain lacunae which were questioned in various High Courts and also the Supreme Court. Therefore, the Act was amended, widening its scope and giving it more teeth. After passing the Recovery of Debts Due to Banks and Financial Institutions (Amendment) Act, 2000, the Supreme Court delivered a comprehensive judgement in Civil Appeal No. 2536 of 2000, dated 16th April 2000 in *Allahabad Bank v. Canara Bank and Another*,[6] dealing with almost all-important provisions of the Act.

The interesting question regarding the impact of the provisions of the Recovery of Debts Due to Banks and Financial Institutions Act, 1993, on the provisions of the Companies Act, 1956 was also discussed by the Hon'ble Supreme Court in the aforesaid case. The dispute was between two nationalised banks: the Allahabad Bank, which had obtained a simple money decree against the debtor company (M/s. M.S. Shoes [East] Co. Ltd) from the Debt Recovery Tribunal at Delhi under the RDB Act, and the Canara Bank, whose claim as a secured creditor was still pending before the same tribunal against the same company. The Allahabad Bank appealed before the Supreme Court against an order passed by the learned company judge under Sections 442 and 537 of the Companies Act, staying the sale proceedings taken out by the Allahabad Bank before the recovery officer under the DRT Act. Applications for winding up the defendant company were pending in the Delhi High Court. The point raised by the respondent Canara Bank was that the appellant Allahabad Bank was obliged to seek leave of the Company Court under the Companies Act, 1956, and the Company Court can stay these proceedings as aforesaid under Sections 442 and 537 for the ultimate purpose of deciding the priorities, in the event of a wind-up order or other order appointing a provisional liquidator being passed under Section 446(1) of the Companies Act, 1956.

The appellant Allahabad Bank contended that the DRT Act was a special statute intended for expeditious adjudication and recovery of debts due to banks and financial institutions and that it contained two crucial provisions.

One of them was Section 18, which ousts the jurisdiction of all courts or other authorities (except the Supreme Court and the High Court exercising powers under Articles 226 and 227) in relation to matters covered by Section 17 and that Section 17 covered the entire procedure from the filing of an application under Section 19 to the adjudication and recovery. The proceedings under the RDB Act could not be stayed by the Company Court nor could they be transferred to the Company Court. No leave of the Company Court was necessary either for the filing of the OA for adjudication of the debt or for executing the decree passed by the Tribunal. Section 34(2) proceedings saved only six statutes from the purview of Section 34(1). The Companies Act, 1956, was not one of them. Hence, the DRT Act, 1993, override Sections 442, 537 and 446 of the Companies Act. It was contended that Section 446 could not be invoked in this case because there was no winding-up order nor an order appointing a provisional liquidator so far. Only Section 529-A of the Companies Act is activated and that too was for the limited purpose of if a question of the "workman's portion" was involved.

As against the arguments of the appellant, the respondent, i.e. Canara Bank, submitted that when a winding-up petition was pending in the Company Court, it was necessary that the leave of the Company Court was obtained for obtaining a decree before the Tribunal or for execution before the recovery officer. Leave was necessary under Section 537, even if no winding-up order was passed. The Company Court alone could sell the properties of the company in the winding-up proceedings. The recovery proceedings must be stayed, and then the proceedings must be transferred to the Company Court, and thereafter, once the proceeds of sale come before the Company Court, the said court alone would have to distribute the monies according to priorities as mentioned in Sections 446(2) (d), 529, 529-A and 530 of the Companies Act, 1956.

The Hon'ble Supreme Court held that the adjudication of liability and the recovery of the amount by execution of the certificate were respectively within the exclusive jurisdiction of the Tribunal and the recovery officer, and no other court or authority, much less the Civil Court or the Company Court, could go into the said questions relating to the liability and the recovery except as provided in the Act. The Hon'ble Court held that the Company Court had no jurisdiction to entertain and adjudicate the claims of banks and financial institutions. On the same parity of reasoning, there was no need for the appellant to seek leave of the Company Court to proceed with its claim before the Debt Recovery Tribunal or in respect of the execution proceedings before the recovery officer. Nor could they be transferred to the Company Court. The Hon'ble Court further held that the purpose of the DRT Act was something more important than the purpose of Sections 442, 446 and 537 of the Companies Act.

Another interesting question regarding the legal complexities relating to the jurisdiction of the DRT to entertain the execution petition when decree of the Civil Court is for more than Rs.10.00 lakhs came up for consideration before the Hon'ble Supreme Court of India in *Punjab National Bank, Dasuya v. Chajju Ram and Others.*[7]

In this case, the appellant filed a suit for recovery of Rs.6, 19,250 in the Civil Court. By judgement dated 16th February 1994, the trial court decreed the suit for the aforesaid amount with interest. In the meanwhile, on 25th June 1993, the Recovery of Debts Due to Banks and Financial Institutions Act, 1993, had come into force. On 18th February 1997, the appellant moved an application before the civil court, Dasuya, for the transfer of the execution proceedings to the DRT, Jaipur. This application was allowed, and the trial court ordered the transfer of the execution proceedings to the DRT, Jaipur. The respondents thereupon filed a revision petition in the High Court. By judgement, the High Court came to the conclusion, while reversing the decision of the trial court, that the execution proceedings could not be transferred and that it was only the Civil Court, which had passed the decree, that could execute the same. Against the said High Court order, an appeal by special leave was filed before the Hon'ble Supreme Court.

The Hon'ble Court held that Section 31 contemplates not only the transfer of a suit but also the transfer of a proceeding which may be other than a suit, like an execution application. When the amount due to the bank under the decree became more than Rs.10 lakhs and an application for execution was filed, it could only be entertained by the DRT and not by the Civil Court. Hence, the Hon'ble Supreme Court allowed the appeal, and the judgement of the High Court was set aside.

II. Challenges faced by the Recovery of Debts Due to Banks and Financial Institutions Act, 1993

For few years, the new dispensation under the Recovery of Debts Due to Banks and Financial Institutions Act, 1993, worked well, and the Presiding Officers appointed to man the tribunals worked with great zeal to ensure that cases involving recovery of the dues of banks and financial institutions were decided expeditiously. However, with the passage of time, the proceedings before the tribunals became synonymous with those of the regular courts and the lawyers representing the borrowers and defaulters used every possible mechanism and dilatory tactics to impede the expeditious adjudication of such cases.

The survey conducted by the Ministry of Finance, Government of India, revealed that in 2001, a sum of more than Rs.1,20,000/crores was due to the banks and financial institutions, and this was adversely affecting the economy of the country. The Narasimham and Andhyarujina Committees have suggested the enactment of new legislation for securitisation and to empowering the banks and financial institutions to take possession and sell the securities without the intervention of the court.

The study showed that as far as India was concerned, the legal impediments and time-consuming nature of the asset disposal process was creating lots of challenges for bankers in resolving the issues pertaining to NPAs. It was also observed that in countries like China, Thailand, Korea and Japan, time consuming, expensive and complicated legal systems are impediments in resolving the issues of NPAs.[8] In the Financial Stability Report[9] by the Reserve Bank of India, it was stated that the effectiveness of various measures to improve the asset quality of banks also depended on the efficient functioning of the DRTs. The shortcomings and loopholes of the Recovery of Debts Due to Banks and Financial Institutions Act had paved the way for the introduction of the Securitisation and Reconstruction of Assets and Enforcement of Security Interest Act in 2002.

III. The backlog of pending cases in Debt Recovery Tribunals

It is a fact that the backlog of pending cases in DRT has doubled in the recent past. The Finance Ministry informed Lok Sabha that the Debt Recovery Tribunals in India had 161,000 cases pending for adjudication as of 28th February 2022.[10] The ministry said the 39 DRTs in the country had, in the year 2018–19, disposed of 24,140 cases and recovered Rs.12,861 crores. These statistics show that while the government and the banking regulator are moving towards stronger debt recovery rules, the process of actual loan recovery remains at slow pace.

Although under the DRT Act, the tribunals were supposed to dispose of a matter referred to it within 180 days of the receipt of an application, the study found that in the rarest of rare cases only the tribunals were able to deliver the order within the stipulated time.

The multiple administrative issues faced by the tribunals is one of the reasons for slow bad loan resolution. There are several DRTs where presiding officers have retired but new ones have yet to be appointed. At some places, the load of pending cases is so high, the tribunals are not able to cope with the pressure. It was found that the repeated appeals that every case goes through is another reason for slow resolution. The best way to see quick movement would be to set a ceiling on appeals, depending on the amount of money involved in each case. More transparency and accountability in the way the cases in tribunals are being dealt with is also necessary.

IV. The constitutional validity of the SARFAESI Act

The constitutional validity of the SARFAESI Act was considered by the Hon'ble Supreme Court of India in the popular case of *Mardia Chemicals Ltd v. Union of India*.[11] The Hon'ble Supreme Court of India upheld the validity of the Act and its provisions except that of Sub-Section (2) of Section 17 of the Act, which was declared *ultra vires* of Article 14 of the Constitution of India. It was also observed in the Mardia Chemicals case that where a secured creditor has taken action under Section 13(4) of the Act, in such cases it would allow borrowers/guarantors to file appeals under Section 17 of the Act within the limitation as prescribed.

1. *After effects of the decision in Mardia Chemicals*

The Act was amended w.e.f. 11.11.2004 in the light of the observations of the Hon'ble Supreme Court in Mardia Chemicals case and the following major amendments to the Act were carried out:

- **Section 3-A** was inserted to provide an opportunity for the borrower to make a representation or raise objections against the demand notice issued under Sub-Section (2) of Section 13 and for the disposal of such representation within 1 week from the date of its receipt. A proviso was inserted that the reasons communicated to the borrower in response to the representation shall not confer any right upon him to prefer an application to the Debt Recovery Tribunal.
- **Sub-Section (2) of Section 17** was amended. Previous sub-section provided that the appeal filed by the borrower against the measures taken by the secured creditor under Sub-Section (4) of Section 13 shall not be entertained unless the borrower deposited with the Debt Recovery Tribunal 75% of the amount claimed under demand notice with a proviso that the Debts Recovery Tribunal may waive or reduce the amount for reasons to be recorded in writing. The new provision removed the condition of deposit of 75% of the amount and substituted with the provision that the Debt Recovery Tribunal shall consider whether any of the measures referred in Sub-Section (4) of Section 13 taken by the secured creditor are in accordance with the provisions of the Act and rules made there under.
- **The provision of appeal to the Appellate Tribunal under Section 18** was also modified accordingly, providing that the Appellate Tribunal shall not entertain any appeal against the order made by the Debts Recovery Tribunal under Section 17 unless 50% of the amount of debt due is deposited with the Appellate Tribunal with a proviso that the Appellate Tribunal is vested with the discretion to reduce the amount to not less than 25% of the debt.
- **The Recovery of Debts Due to Banks and Financial Institutions Act** was also amended to include a proviso to Section 19 (1) to the effect that the bank or financial institution may, with the permission of the Debts Recovery Tribunal, withdraw the application whether made before or after the Enforcement of Security Interest and Recovery of Debt Laws (Amendment) Act, 2004, for the purposes of taking action under the SARFAESI Act.

2. *Classification of account as NPA-legal validity*

The classification of the account of the borrowers as 'NPA' by banks under the SARFAESI Act was taken up as an issue of dispute between the banks and the borrowers in various courts/judicial forums. Several rounds of litigation have happened on this issue at various courts across the country. Ultimately, the Hon'ble Supreme Court of India settled this issue in its judgement delivered on 28th January 2015 in *Keshavlal Khemchand and Sons Pvt. Ltd v. Union of India & Others*,[12] by upholding the constitutional validity of the amended definition of the expression NPA under Section 2(1)(o) of the SARFAESI Act.

The original definition of NPA as given under the provisions of the SARFAESI Act, 2002, and the amended definition of NPA after the Amendment Act passed in 2004, which is now under challenge, are in Table 3.1 for a better understanding of the issue.

While challenging the constitutionality of the amended definition of the expression 'NPA' under Section 2(1)(o) of the SARFAESI Act, the borrowers raised *inter alia* the following contentions before the Hon'ble Supreme Court of India:

(1) The Parliament abdicated its essential legislative function by authorising the various bodies to frame guidelines in accordance with which the account of the borrower could be classified as NPA.

Table 3.1 Original definition of NPA as given under the provisions of the SARFAESI Act, 2002, and the amended definition of NPA after the Amendment Act passed in 2004.

Definition of NPA as under SARFAESI Act, 2002	*Definition of NPA after SARFAESI Amendment Act, 2004*
Section 2(1) (o) – "non-performing asset" means an asset or account of a borrower, which has been classified by a bank or financial institution as sub-standard, doubtful or loss asset in accordance with the directions or under guidelines relating to assets classifications issued by the Reserve Bank.	Section 2(1) (o) – "non-performing asset" means an asset or account of a borrower, which has been classified by a bank or financial institution as sub-standard, doubtful or loss asset - (a) in case such bank or financial institution is administered or regulated by any authority or body established, constituted or appointed by any law for the time being in force, in accordance with the directions or guidelines relating to assets classifications issued by such authority or body; (b) in any other case, in accordance with the directions or guidelines relating to assets classifications issued by the Reserve Bank.

(2) The amended definition of NPA enables different creditors to adopt different guidelines which prescribe different standards for arriving at a conclusion that the account of a borrower is NPA.
(3) The SARFAESI Act does not provide for a reasonable opportunity to demonstrate that the classification of the borrower's account as NPA is untenable, the power to make such a classification itself becomes arbitrary and is a violation of Article 14 of the Constitution.

In responding to these contentions, the Union of India, RBI and bankers took the following stand before the Hon'ble Supreme Court of India:

(1) Because the assessment of the account of borrower as NPA depends upon innumerable factors which constantly keep changing, Parliament thought it fit to stipulate that the assessment be made in light of the guidelines made by either the RBI or various other regulators regulating the activities of various creditors. Hence, there is no delegation of any essential legislative functions.
(2) The classification of NPA on the basis of the guidelines framed by different bodies regulating the different creditors is a constitutionally permissible classification having regard to the nature of the different credit facilities extended by various creditors to different categories of borrowers and on different terms and conditions.

During the course of arguments, the Reserve Bank of India submitted that prior to the amendments in 2004, NPA was defined as a sub-standard, doubtful or loss asset in accordance with the directions or under guidelines relating to assets classification issued by the Reserve Bank. Irrespective of whether the financial entity was regulated by RBI or not, for the purposes of SARFAESI Act, the asset classification stipulated by RBI was applicable. Though the regulator concerned with the financial entity had stipulated different standards for regulatory purposes, the entities had to apply the criteria stipulated by RBI for asset classification so far as the SARFAESI Act was concerned. The amendment brought in 2004 addressed this issue and brought uniformity to the classification of assets by financial entities, both for the purposes of complying with the directions issued by their own regulations and for the purposes of SARFAESI Act. Thus, the amendment in 2004 ruled out a situation where an asset is not an NPA as per the specifications of the regulator, but the same asset is an NPA for the purposes of the SARFAESI Act or vice versa.

The Department of Financial Services, Ministry of Finance also submitted before the Hon'ble Court that the amendments were made in 2004 to ensure that the guidelines issued by the concerned regulator are covered for the purpose of recovery under the SARFAESI Act. It further submitted that there are financial institutions, such as Housing Finance Corporations, which are regulated by the National Housing Bank. The non-performing assets of these institutions are classified per the guidelines prescribed by National Housing Bank. The amendment covered the entities regulated by different regulators such as RBI, National Housing Bank, and the Asian Development Bank. Therefore, the amendments were necessary to cover the deficiencies noticed in the SARFAESI Act.

Taking into account of the arguments extended on behalf of RBI, Ministry of Finance and the bankers, the Hon'ble Supreme Court of India held that the allegations of the borrowers that the SARFAESI Act did not provide for a reasonable opportunity to demonstrate that the classification of the borrower's account as NPA fails on the express language of Section 13(3A), which obligated the secured creditors (banks) to examine the representation/objection made by the borrower and communicate the reasons for non-acceptance of the representation or objections to the borrowers. In view of the aforesaid observations, the Hon'ble Supreme Court upheld that the amended definition of the expression "NPA" under Section 2(1)(o) of the Act was constitutionally valid. Accordingly, the Hon'ble Supreme Court allowed the appeals filed by the creditors/banks and also directed each petitioner/borrower to pay costs to the respective creditors/banks calculated at 1% of the amount outstanding on the date of notice under Section 13(2) of the Act in each of the cases.

The legal validity of the provisions relating to the classification of the account as NPA and the RBI guidelines on this aspect was also considered by the Hon'ble High Court of Madras in M/s. *Decan Chronicles Holdings Limited v. Union of India and Others.*[13] The Hon'ble Court observed that what is required to be seen is the intention of the Legislature at the time of enactment. In this case, the Legislature left the job of defining a non-performing asset in the hands of the Reserve Bank of India. The Reserve Bank of India issued the Master Circular on NPA after taking into consideration the global economy, the prevailing situation, and the intention to create transparency and uniformity with the banking system in order to provide stability and to protect the interests of depositors. When such a decision has been made based upon analysis of material factors, the same cannot be set aside as arbitrary.

The Reserve Bank of India laid down a policy that provided guidelines for declaring an asset to be a non-performing asset. The policy, known as "RBIs Prudential norms on Income Recognition, Asset Classification and Provisioning Pertaining to Advances", was published in a circular dated 30th August 2001. In the circular, it says:

> 1.1 In line with the international practices and as per the recommendations made by the Committee on the Financial System (Chairman Shri M. Narasimham), the Reserve Bank of India has introduced, in a phased manner, prudential norms for income recognition, asset classification and provisioning for the advances portfolio of the banks so as to move towards greater consistency and transparency in the published accounts.

In Section 2.1 of the policy, it says the following about non-performing assets, "2.1.1 An asset, including a leased asset, becomes non-performing when it ceases to generate income for the bank". A non-performing asset was defined as a credit facility in respect of which the interest and/or instalment of principal has remained past due for a specified period of time. Hence, a Non-Performing Asset (NPA) shall be an advance where:

(i) interest and/or instalment of principal remain overdue for a period of more than 180 days in respect of a Term Loan,
(ii) the account remains out of order for a period of more than 180 days, in respect of an Overdraft/Cash Credit (OD/CC),
(iii) the bill remains overdue for a period of more than 180 days in the case of bills purchased and discounted,
(iv) interest and/or instalment of principal remains overdue for two harvest seasons but for a period not exceeding two and half years in the case of an advance granted for agricultural purposes, and
(v) any amount to be received remains overdue for a period of more than 180 days in respect of other accounts. Subsequently as per the instructions of RBI, 180 days was reduced to 90 days).

In Section 4.2.2 of the policy, it states

> Banks should establish appropriate internal systems to eliminate the tendency to delay or postpone the identification of NPAs, especially in respect of high value accounts. The banks may fix a minimum cut off point to decide what would constitute a high value account depending upon their respective business levels. The cut off point should be valid for the entire accounting year. Responsibility and validation levels for ensuring proper asset classification may be fixed by the banks. The system should ensure that doubts in asset classification due to any reason are settled through specified internal channels within one month from the date on which the account would have been classified as NPA as per extant guidelines.

The Hon'ble Court held that from what is quoted here, the Reserve Bank of India laid down the terms and conditions and circumstances in which the debt was to be classified as a non-performing asset, and hence there is no substance in the submission made on behalf of the petitioners that there are no guidelines for treating the debt as a non-performing asset.

It is relevant to add that the Narasimham Committee also advocated for a legal framework to more clearly define the rights and liabilities of the parties to the contract and provisions for speedy resolution of disputes, which is a *sine qua non* for efficient trade and commerce, especially for financial intermediation. Even the guidelines of the Reserve Bank of India says that in relation to classifying the NPAs, a system must be evolved to ensure that the doubts in asset classification are settled or resolved through specified internal channels within the time specified in the guidelines. The circular also provided for the sale of the financial assets on a 'without recourse' basis, and the banks were directed to ensure that the effect of the sale of the financial assets should be such that the asset is taken off the books of the bank, and after the sale there should not be any known liability devolving to the banks. The guideline procedure for the sale of a bank's financial assets to the securitisation/reconstruction companies was laid down by the Reserve Bank of India in the Master Circular issued on 1 July 2014.[14]

3. *Mechanism to resolve legal issues – challenges*

With regard to the mechanism to resolve the issues relating to classification of accounts as non-performing assets, in terms of Section 13(3A) of the Act, the borrower/guarantor is entitled to submit objections and representations. The purpose of serving a notice upon the borrower under Sub-Section (2) of Section 13 of the Act is that a reply may be submitted by the borrower explaining the reasons as to why measures may or may not be taken under Sub-Section (4) of Section 13 in cases of non-compliance of notice within 60 days. The authorised officer is legally bound to consider the objections raised in reply to such notice, and an internal mechanism must be particularly evolved to consider such objections raised in the reply to the notice.

In terms of the judgement of the Hon'ble Supreme Court in the Mardia Chemicals case, there must be some meaningful consideration of the objections raised rather than to ritually reject them and proceed to take drastic measures under Sub-Section (4) of Section 13 of the Act. Once such a duty is envisaged on the part of the creditor, it would only be conducive to the principles of fairness on the part of the banks and financial institutions in dealing with their borrowers to apprise them of the reason for not accepting the objections or points raised in reply to the notice served upon them before proceeding to take measures under Sub-Section (4) of Section 13. Such reasons, overruling the objections of the borrower, must also be communicated to the borrower by the secured creditor.

While stressing the need for proper consideration of the objections of the borrowers/guarantors, the Hon'ble Court also made it unequivocally clear that the communication of the reasons for not accepting the objections presented by the secured borrower may not be taken to give an occasion to resort to such proceedings that are not permissible under the provisions of the Act. But the communication of reasons for not accepting the objections of the borrower would certainly be for the purpose of his knowledge, which would be a step forward towards his right to know why his objections were not accepted by the secured creditor who intended to resort to the harsh steps of taking over the management/business of viz. secured assets without the intervention of the Court. Such a person, in respect of whom steps under Section 13(4) of the Act are likely to be taken, cannot be denied the right to know the reason of non-acceptance of his objections. It is true that per the provisions of the Act, he may not be entitled to challenge the reasons communicated or the likely action of the secured creditor at that point of time unless his right to approach the Debt Recovery Tribunal as provided under Section 17 of the Act matures on any measures taken under Sub-Section (4) of Section 13 of the Act.

4. *Importance of communicating reasons for rejection of representation/objection under Section 3 (3A) of SARFAESI Act*

In terms of Section 3 (3A) of the SARFAESI Act, it is necessary to communicate the reasons for not accepting the objections raised by the borrower in reply to notice under Section 13(2) of the Act. Therefore, it goes with logic and reason that the borrower/guarantor may communicate the reason for not accepting the objections if they are raised and before taking measures such as taking over possession of the secured assets.

This would also be in line with the concept of a right to know and the lenders' liability of fairness to keep the borrower informed, particularly of the developments immediately before taking measures under Sub-Section (4) of Section 13 of the Act. It would also cater to the cause of transparency and would be conducive in building an atmosphere of confidence and healthy commercial practices. Such a duty is inherent under Section 13(2) of the Act.

5. *Right to file an appeal before DRT*

The next safeguard available to a secure borrower within the framework of the Act is to approach the Debt Recovery Tribunal under Section 17 of the Act. Such a right exists only after measures are taken under Sub-Section (1) of Section 13 of the Act. Section 13 of the Act leaves more scope and provides wider protections to the borrower compared to cases of an English mortgage. In an English mortgage, there is no scope of intervention for the court unless a case is made out before the court that the action of the mortgagee is fraudulent or case of a similar nature. Otherwise, as provided under Sub-Section (3) of Section 69, a mortgagor shall only be entitled to the damages for the wrongful or irregular sale of the property. Whereas under the securitisation rules it is provided that before putting the property on sale the authorised officer has to obtain the valuation of immovable property, a reserved price is to be fixed and a notice of 30 days before the sale is to be served on the borrower. In this connection, Rule 9, the relevant rule, of the Security Interest (Enforcement) Rules, 2002 is quoted next:

> "9. Time of sale, issues of sale certificate and delivery of possession, etc.
>
> (1) No sale of immovable property under these rules, in first instance shall take place before the expiry of thirty days from the date on which

the public notice of sale is published in newspapers as referred to in the proviso to sub-Rule (6) or notice of sale has been served to the borrower:

Provided further that if sale of immovable property by any one of the methods specified by sub-rule (5) of rule 8 fails and sale is required to be conducted again, the authorised officer shall serve, affix and publish notice of sale of not less than fifteen days to the borrower, for any subsequent sale.

(2) The sale shall be confirmed in favour of the purchaser who has offered the highest sale price in his bid or tender or quotation or offer to the authorized officer and shall be subject to confirmation by the secured creditor . . .".

46. Therefore, during this period which would be more than 60 days it would be open for a borrower to approach the Debt Recovery Tribunal and file a petition for any appropriate relief and if a case is so made out, he can even get a relief of stay, in exercise of ancillary power which vest in the Tribunal as per decisions referred and ITO v. Mohd Kunhi[15] and, Allahabad Bank v. Radha Krishna Maity.[16]

47. In terms of Section 19 of the Act, if the Tribunal finds that the secured assets have been wrongfully transferred or taken possession, an order for return of such assets can be passed and the borrower in that even shall also be entitled for compensation.

A full reading of Section 34 shows that the jurisdiction of the civil court is barred in respect of matters to which a Debt Recovery Tribunal or Appellate Tribunal is empowered to determine any action taken "or to be taken in pursuance of any power conferred under this Act". In this context, the judgement of the Hon'ble High Court of Calcutta in M/s. *Mercury Exporters and Manufacturing Pvt. Ltd & Another v. Punjab National Bank and Another*,[17] is worth mentioning. The Hon'ble Calcutta High Court held that the borrowers/guarantors can approach the Debt Recovery Tribunal under Section 17(1) of the Act only after possession of the secured asset is lost by the borrower/guarantor.

6. *Appellate proceedings – A misnomer*

In terms of judgements of various courts, the proceedings under Section 17 of the Act are not appellate proceedings, and it is a misnomer. In fact, it is the initial action which is brought before a forum as prescribed under the Act, raising grievances against the action or measures taken by one of the parties to the contract. It is the stage of an initial proceeding like filing a suit in civil court. As a matter of fact, proceedings under Section 17 of the Act are in lieu of a civil suit in which a remedy is ordinarily available but for the bar under Section 34 of the Act in the present case.

The Hon'ble Court referred to the decision in Smt. *Ganga Bai v. Vijay Kumar*[18] where in respect of the original and appellate proceedings a distinction was drawn as follows:

> "15 . . . There is a basic distinction between the right of suit and the right of appeal. There is an inherent right in every person to bring a suit of civil nature and unless the suit is barred by statute one may, at ones peril, bring a suit of one's choice. It is no answer to a suit, howsoever frivolous to claim, that the law confers no such right to sue. A suit for its maintainability requires no authority of law and it is enough that no statute bars the suit. But the position in regard to appeals is quite the opposite. The right of appeal inheres in no one and, therefore, an appeal for its maintainability must have the clear authority of law. That explains why the right of appeal is described as a creature of statute".
>
> (p. 397)

7. *Pre-deposit of 75% for filing appeal*

The Hon'ble Supreme Court in Mardia Chemicals case[19] held that the amount of deposit of 75% of the demand at the initial proceeding itself sounded unreasonable and oppressive, more particularly when the secured assets/the management thereof along with the right to transfer such interest was taken over by the secured creditor or, in some cases, property was also sold. The requirement of a deposit of such a large amount on the basis of a one-sided claim alone cannot be said to be a reasonable condition at the first instance itself before the start of the adjudication of the dispute. Merely giving power to the Tribunal to waive or reduce the amount did not cure the inherent infirmity leaning one-sidedly in favour of the party, who, so far was alone the party to decide the amount and the fact of default and classifying the dues as NPAs without participation/association of the borrower in the process. Such an onerous and oppressive condition should not be left operative in the expectation of a reasonable exercise of discretion by the concerned authority. Placed in a situation as indicated earlier, where it may not be possible for the borrower to raise any amount to make the deposit, his secured assets having already been taken possession of or sold, such a rider to approach the Tribunal at the first instance of proceedings, captioned as an appeal, rendered the remedy illusory and nugatory.

As indicated earlier, the position of the appeal under Section 17 of the Act is like that of a suit in the court of the first instance under the Code of Civil Procedure. No doubt in suits also it is permissible, in given facts and circumstances and under the provisions of the law, to attach the property before a decree is passed or to appoint a receiver and to make a provision by way of an interim measure in respect of the property in suit. But for obtaining such orders a case for the same is to be made out in accordance with the relevant provisions under the law. There is no such provision under the Act.

The justification given by banks/FIs regarding the requirement of a pre-deposit is that the secured assets, which may be taken possession of or sold, may fall short of the dues; therefore, such a deposit may be necessary. However, the Hon'ble Court found no merit in this submission. In such an eventuality, the recourse may have to be taken to Sub-Section 10 of Section 13 where a petition may have to be filed before the Tribunal for the purpose of making up the shortfall.

The condition of pre-deposit in the present case was a bad rendering the remedy, which was illusory on the grounds that (i) it was imposed while approaching the adjudicating authority of the first instance, not in the appeal; (ii) there was no determination of the amount due as yet; (iii) the secured assets or its management with transferable interest was already taken over and under the control of the secured creditor; (iv) there was no special reason for a double security in respect to an amount yet to be determined and settled; (v) 75% of the amount claimed would by no means be a meagre amount; and (vi) it would leave the borrower in a position where it would not be possible for him to raise any funds to make deposit of 75% of the undetermined demand. Such conditions are not just onerous and oppressive but also unreasonable and arbitrary. Accordingly, the Hon'ble Supreme Court held that Sub-Section (2) of Section 17 of the Act as unreasonable, arbitrary and in violation of Article 14 of the Constitution.

8. *Public interest versus private interest*

One of the contentions that has been forcefully raised against the SARFAESI Act is that the existing rights of private parties under a contract cannot be interfered with by putting one party to an advantageous position over the other. For example, in the matter of a private contract between the borrower and the financing bank or institution, through impugned legislation, the rights of the borrowers have been curtailed and the enforcement of secured assets has been provided for without intervention of the court, which above all deprives them of the remedy available under the law by approaching a civil court. Such a law, it is submitted, is not envisaged in any civilised society governed by the rule of law.

The Hon'ble Supreme Court held in Mardia Chemicals[20] case that although the transaction may have had a character of a private contract, the question of great importance behind such transactions as a whole has a far reaching effect on the economy of the country and cannot be ignored, by purely restricting it to individual transactions, more particularly when financing is through banks and financial institutions that are utilising the money of the people in general, namely the depositors in the banks and the public money at the disposal of the financial institutions. Therefore, wherever public interest to such a large extent is involved and it may become necessary to achieve an objective that serves the public purposes, individual rights may have to give way. Public interest has always been considered to be above private interest. The interest of an individual may, to some extent, be affected, but it cannot have the potential to take over the public interest, which would have an impact on the socio-economic drive of the country. The two aspects are inter-twined, which is difficult to separated. There have been many instances where the existing rights of individuals have been affected by legislative measures taken in public interest. In *Ramaswamy Aiyengar v. Kailasa Thevar*,[21] by enacting the Madras Agriculturalists Relief Act, relief was given to the debtors, who were agriculturists as a class, by sealing down their debts. The validity of the Act was upheld, although it affected the individual interest of creditors.

In the *Dahya Lal v. Rasul Mohd. Abdul Rahim*[22] (1963) 3 SCR 1, the tenants under the Provisions of the Bombay Tenancy Act, 1939, were given protection against eviction, and they were granted the status of a protected tenant who had cultivated the land personally 6 years prior to the prescribed date. It was found that the legislation was with the objective of improving the economic conditions of the peasants and to ensure full and efficient use of land for agricultural purposes. In the case of *Kanshi Ram v. Lachhman*[23] (2001) 5 SCC 546, the law granting relief to the debtors protecting their property was upheld.

The Hon'ble Court further held that in the present case, the unrealised dues of banking companies and financial institutions were mounting, and it was considered imperative in view of recommendations of the expert committees to have a law that may provide a speedier remedy for the recovery of bank's dues. Such legislation would be in the public interest, and the individual interest would be subservient to it. Even if a few borrowers were affected here and there, that would not impinge upon the validity of the Act that otherwise serves the larger interest.

9. *Independent adjudicatory authority*

Another major contention against the SARFAESI Act is that no adjudicatory mechanism is available to the borrower to ventilate his grievance through an independent adjudicatory authority. Access to justice is the hallmark of our judicial system. Section 34 of the Act bars the jurisdiction of the civil courts to entertain a suit in matters of the recovery of loans. The remedy of appeal available under the Act as contained in Section 17 can be availed only after measures have already been taken by the secured creditor under Sub-Section (4) of Section 13 of the Act which includes sale of the secured assets, taking over its management and all transferable rights thereto. Before filing an appeal under section 17 of the Act, decision is to be taken in respect of all matters by the bank or financial institution itself which can hardly be said to be an independent agency rather they are a party to the transaction having unilateral power to initiate action under sub-Section (4) of section 13 of the Act. The remedy under Article 226 of the Constitution of India may not always be available since the dispute may be only between two private parties, the banking companies, co-operative banks or financial institutions, or foreign banks, some of them may not be authorities within the meaning of Article 12 of the Constitution of India against whom a writ petition could be maintainable. Thus the position that emerged is that a borrower was virtually left with no remedy. Where access to the court is prohibited and no proper adjudicatory mechanism is provided, such a law is unconstitutional and cannot survive.[24] Some adjudicatory processes through an independent agency is essential for determining the rights of the parties, more particularly when the consequences that flow from the offending Act defeat the civil rights of a party.[25]

On the other hand, the counsels for bankers argued that in a contractual matter between the two private parties they are supposed to act in terms of the contract and no question of compliance with the principles of natural justice arises nor does the question of a judicial review of such actions needs to be provided for. However, the Hon'ble Court held in the Mardia Chemicals case[26] that the contract that has been entered into between the two private parties in some respects has been superseded by the statutory provisions, or it may be said that such contracts are now governed by the statutory provisions relating to recovery of debts and bar the jurisdiction of the civil court to entertain any disputes in respect of such matters.

After taking into consideration all the aspects involved in the case, the Hon'ble Supreme Court upheld all the provisions of the SARFAESI Act, except the requirement of a deposit of 75% of the amount claimed before entertaining an appeal (petition). The Hon'ble Court held that Section 17 of the Act put up oppressive, onerous and arbitrary conditions against all the canons of reasonableness and it struck down the same.

The Hon'ble Court further held that the borrowers would get a reasonably fair deal and the opportunity to get the matter adjudicated upon before the Debt Recovery Tribunal. The effect of some of the provisions may be a bit harsh for some of the borrowers, but on that ground the impugned provisions of the Act cannot be said to be unconstitutional in view of the fact that the objective of the Act is to achieve a speedier recovery of the dues declared as NPAs and a better availability of capital liquidity and resources to help in the growth of the country's economy and the welfare of the people in general, which would subserve the public interest.

Accordingly, the Hon'ble High Court upheld the validity of the Act and its provisions except that of Sub-Section (2) of Section 17 of the Act, which was declared *ultra vires* of Article 14 of the Constitution of India. The Hon'ble Court further observed that where a secured creditor had taken action under Section 13(4) of the Act, it would be open to borrowers to file appeals under Section 17 of the Act within the limitation as prescribed and then, therefore, to be counted with an effect from the date of the judgement.

V. The challenges subsequent to the enactment of the Securitisation and Reconsturction of Financial Assets and Enforcement of Security Interest Act, 2002

In the course of development of recovery laws pertaining to banks, the SARFAESI Act gains more importance and acceptance. However, it also faces a number of challenges from different quarters, primarily on the following grounds:

1. *Arbitrary powers to banks*

The main contention of the those who are challenging the vires of certain provisions of the Act is that the banks and the financial institutions have been vested with arbitrary powers, without any guidelines for its exercise and without providing any appropriate and adequate mechanism to decide the disputes relating to the correctness of the demand, its validity and the actual amount of dues sought to be recovered from the borrowers. The offending provisions of the Act have been made one-sided affair while enforcing drastic measures of the sale of the property or taking over the management or the possession of the secured assets without affording any opportunity to the borrower.

In fact, the contention of the critics of SARFAESI is that there was no occasion to enact such a draconian legislation to find a short cut to realise the dues without their ascertainment but in which the secured creditor considered to be the dues and declare the same as NPAs. Out of the total NPAs that are considered to be about 1 lakh crores, about half of them are due against priority sectors like agriculture, etc. The dues between 10 lakhs to 1 crore constitute only 13.90% of the total dues. Further, there is already a special enactment providing for the recovery of dues of banks and financial institutions. Therefore, it was not necessary to enact yet another legislation containing drastic steps and procedures depriving the debtors of any fair opportunities to defend themselves from the onslaught of the harsh steps as provided under the Act.

2. *No provisions for lenders liability*

Another criticism against the SARFAESI Act was that no provision has been made to take into account the lenders' liability, although at one time it was considered necessary to have an enactment relating to lenders' liability, and a bill was also intended to be introduced, as it was considered necessary for the lenders to conduct themselves responsibly towards the borrowers. It is submitted that despite such a statement, as indicated earlier, on the floor of the House, no such laws have been enacted so far, nor has any care been taken to introduce such safeguards in the Act to protect the borrowers against their vulnerability to arbitrary or irresponsible action on the part of the lenders.

On a comparative basis, in relation to other countries, the percentage of NPA against the GDP is only 6% in India, which is much less compared to China, Malaysia, Thailand, Japan, South Korea and other countries. Therefore, it is evident that this resort was taken for drastic legislation under the misapprehension that other ways and means have failed to recover the dues from the borrowers.

3. Non-adjudicatory and non-judicial

The judicial proceeding without the intervention of the court is an issue which has been vehemently opposed by the persons who are advocating against the provisions of the SARFAESI Act. Their contention is that a security interest can be enforced by the secured creditor straightaway, without the intervention of the court, on default in repayment of an instalment and non-compliance of a notice of 60 days, declaring the loan as a non-performing asset. Under Sub-Section 4 of Section 13, the secured creditor is entitled to take possession of the secured assets and may transfer them by way of a lease, assignment or sale as provided under Clause (a) or under Clause (b) to take over the management of the secured assets including the right to transfer any secured assets or to appoint any person as provided in Clause (c) to manage the secured assets taken over by the creditor. Under Clause (d), by means of a notice any person who has acquired any of the secured assets from the borrower, or who has to pay to the borrower any amount that may cover the secured debt, can be asked to pay it to the secured creditor. All that is provided is that if all the dues with costs and charges and expenses incurred by the creditor are tendered before the date fixed for the sale of the assets, no further steps shall be taken for the sale of the property.

It is submitted that the mechanism provided for recovery of the debt under Section 13 does not provide for any adjudicatory forum to resolve any disputes that may arise in relation to the liability of the borrower to be treated as a defaulter or to see if there has been any violation or lapse on the part of the creditor or in regard to the correctness of the amount sought to be recovered and the interest levied thereupon. On the other hand, Section 34 bars the jurisdiction of the civil court to entertain any suit in respect of any matter that a Debt Recovery Tribunal or the Appellate Tribunal is empowered to determine. It also provides that no injunction shall be granted by any court or other authority in respect of any action taken or to be taken in pursuance of any power conferred by or under the Act or under the Recovery of Debts Due to Banks and Financial Institutions Act, 1993. Section 35 gives an overriding effect for the provisions of the Act over the provisions contained under any other law. So, in effect, before any action is taken under Section 13, there is no forum or adjudicatory mechanism to resolve any disputes that may arise in respect to the alleged dues or the NPA.

4. *Appeal provision is only illusory*

Many critics of the SARFAESI Act are of the view that the provision of appeal as contained in Section 17 of the Act is also illusory since an appeal may be preferred within the specified time from the date on which measures under Sub-Section 4 of Section 13 have been taken. The appeal would be maintainable after the possession of the property, the management of the secured assets has been taken over, or the property has been sold.

Further, an appeal is not entertainable unless 75% of the amount claimed in the notice is deposited by the borrower with the Debt Recovery Tribunal. It would be a matter of the discretion of the Debt Recovery Tribunal to waive the condition of a pre-deposit or to reduce the amount for reasons to be recorded. It is submitted that a remedy that is available, after the damage is done and on fulfilment of such an onerous condition as the deposit of 75% of the demand, is illusory and a mere farce. It is not a real remedy that is available to a borrower before he is subjected to harsh steps as provided under Sub-Section (4) of Section 13. It is further submitted that after the possession of the secured assets, its management has been taken over by the secured creditor, or the property is leased out or sold to any other person, it would not be possible to raise and deposit 75% of the amount claimed by the secured creditor. It is also submitted that once the secured assets are taken over there is hardly any occasion for the deposit of 75% of the claim since it is already secured and the management and possession of the secured assets move into the hands of the creditor. The position thus is that the borrower is gagged into a helpless position where he cannot air his grievances against the drastic steps taken against him. The doors of the civil court are closed to him, and no adjudicatory mechanism is provided before steps are taken under Sub-Section (4) of Section 13. Such a law, it is submitted, is arbitrary and suffers from the vice of unreasonableness.

In so far it relates to Section 19 of the Act, which deals with cases where it is found that possession of the secured assets was wrongfully taken by the secured creditor, he may be directed to return the secured assets to the borrower who may also be entitled to such compensation as determined by the Debt Recovery Tribunal or the Appellate Tribunal. It is submitted that it is hardly a consolation after harsh steps as provided under Sub-Section 4 of Section 13 have been taken.

The contentions against Section 17(2) of the SARFAESI Act were considered positively by the Hon'ble Supreme Court in the Mardia Chemicals[27] case and struck down by declaring it unconstitutional and against the principles of natural justice.

5. *Non-availability of an adjudicatory forum*

The critics of SARFAESI Act are of the view that for exercise of power under Section 13, certain enquiries would be necessary as to whether a person to whom notice is given is under a liability to pay or the extent of the liability, etc. Further the questions pertain to the law of limitation and bar under consortium agreements claim of a set-off/counter-claim, the creditor's defaults as bailee or its failure to disburse the credit in time, the changeability of penal interest or compound interest, the non-appropriation of amount already paid, and so on and so forth. Further the bar of Section 22 of the Sick Industrial Companies Act (hereinafter referred to as SICA) also need to be considered. However, there is no adjudicatory body provided under the SARFAESI Act for dealing with such disputes or adjudication of such disputes.

The power that is exercised by the authorised officer to enforce security by way of sale, etc. without any determination of disputed questions, under Section 13 of the Act, is unconstitutional. The SARFAESI Act has vested the authorised officer with the approval to exercise power without any determination of disputed questions; excluding the judicial remedies renders the Act procedurally and substantively unfair, unreasonable and arbitrary. The power of judicial determination is a manifestation of sovereign power to determine the legal rights, which cannot be vested in private bodies such as foreign banks, co-operative banks or non-banking financial institutions, etc.

The critics pointed out that the scope of Section 13 of the Act is fundamentally different from the scope of power under Section 69 of the Transfer of Property Act. The power under Section 69 of the Transfer of Property Act is hedged with various restrictions to prevent the abuse of power including mortgagors' right to have recourse to court both before and after the sale.[28] Further, even in case of an English mortgage, it is in the nature of conveyance or absolute transfer of mortgage property with provision of retransfer upon the discharge of mortgage. While adequate restrictions were provided under the Transfer of Property Act to protect the interest of the rightful owners of the property, the same care and caution is not provided under the SARFAESI Act.

The scope of Section 13 of the Act is fundamentally different from the scope of power under Section 69 of the Transfer of Property Act. In terms of 2(f) of the SARFAESI Act, the definition of the word "borrower" covers even the guarantor. Section 135 of the Contract Act dealt with instances where a guarantor is discharged of his obligation. In view of the bar of Section 34 to file a suit in the civil court, it is not possible for a guarantor to approach the court to show and establish that he is a discharged guarantor.[29]

Another lacuna is that the word "security" has not been defined under Section 2 of the Act. It is submitted that the Act does not apply to the legal liens. It is submitted that if property is subject to several charges, such as first charge, second charge, and third charge and so on, property in relation to only one of them would be NPA and not in relation to other creditors having charge over the property. It is submitted that it is not clear in such a situation how the Act will be workable. Another instance is Section 44 of the Transfer of Property Act which deals with the case of a transfer by one co-owner and the difficulty of working out the provisions of the Act in such cases.

However, the banks are defending the allegations by stating that the financial institutions are badly affected by non-recovery of dues and despite the existing laws like the Recovery of Debts Due to Banks and Financial Institutions Act, much could not be achieved; hence it was necessary to take further legislative steps to accelerate the recovery of the heavy amount of dues. They contended that after availing the facility of financial assistance quite often, the borrowers hardly show interest in the repayment of the loans, which keep on accumulating, and, as a result, it becomes difficult for the financial institutions to continue extending financial assistance to deserving parties due to the heavy blockade of money stuck with the erring borrowers. It is not good for a financial institution to have heavy NPAs. They further indicated that after the enforcement of the Act, there has been a marked improvement in the recovery and quite a substantial amount has since been recovered.

The banks further content that the Act was enacted to curb the menace of growing NPAs. It affects the banks and financial institutions that are ultimately against the public interest. Due to non-recovery of the dues, the banks also run out of the financial resources to further carry on the financial activities and to meet the needs and requirements of its other depositors and clients. After the Recovery of Debts Due to Banks and Financial Institutions Act and the establishment of the Debt Recovery Tribunals, the success in recovery has not been very encouraging. Therefore, a need was felt for a faster procedure empowering the secured creditors to recover their dues and for securitisation of financial assets to generate maximum monetary liquidity. After the Act came into force, there has been a marked difference in the realisation of dues and more borrowers are coming forward to pay the defaulted amount and clear the dues.

The bankers further highlight that if a defaulter wants to raise any objection, it may be raised in reply to the notice which would obviously be considered by the secured creditor before it would further proceed to take recourse to Sub-Section 4 of Section 13 of the Act. It is further submitted that there will be ample time for a borrower to approach the Debt Recovery Tribunal to seek relief before the sale of the secured assets. The remedy as provided under Section 17 of the Act is adequate. The bar of jurisdiction of the civil court was thought to be necessary to avoid a lengthy legal process in realising the amount due. It is further stated that normally there should be a presumption in favour of the validity of legislation more so in regard to the laws relating to economic and financial matters, and a few instances here and there of any harsh results would not be a valid consideration to invalidate the law.

VI. Recent development in the SARFAESI/DRT Act

As a consequence of the judgement of the Hon'ble Supreme Court in the Mardia Chemicals case, the SARFAESI Act was amended by the Union of India. The condition for a pre-deposit of 75% of the amount claimed in the notice was removed and the borrowers and guarantors have the right to file an appeal before the DRT without a deposit of any amount.

The Enforcement of Security Interest and Recovery of Debts Laws (Amendment) Bill, 2011, was passed by both the Houses of the Parliament, i.e. Lok Sabha and Raja Sabha. The Bill also received assent of the president of India on 3rd January 2013 and became an act (Act No.1 of 2013). Thereafter, many amendments were incorporated into the Act by way of various Amendment Acts, the last being the Enforcement of Security Interest and Recovery of Debts Laws and Miscellaneous Provisions (Amendment) Act, 2016. These acts amended the provisions of the Securitisation and Reconstruction of Financial Assets and Enforcement of Security Interest Act, 2002, and the Recovery of Debts Due to Banks and Financial Institutions Act, 1993. The important highlights of the Amendment Acts are in Tables 3.2 and 3.3.

Table 3.2 Comparison of the provisions before and after the SARFAESI Amendment Act.

Before the amendment of the SARFAESI Act	*After the amendment of the SARFAESI Act*
The banks and financial institutions were required to consider representations from borrowers and communicate their response within a period of *7 days*.	The period within which the response is to be sent to the representation of the borrower is enhanced from *7 days* to *15 days* (Section 13[3A]).
The banks were not empowered to participate in the bid for purchase of any immovable property in realisation of the claim against the defaulted borrower in situations where banks were unable to find a suitable buyer for such assets.	Where the sale of immovable property has been postponed for want of a bid of an amount not less than the reserve price, any officer of the bank may bid on behalf of the bank (Section 13[5A][5B][5C]).
There was no provision for filing a caveat against a SARFAESI application/appeal.	The secured creditor (bank) or any person may lodge a caveat in anticipation of the SARFAESI application/appeal by the borrower/guarantor (Section 18[C]).
There was no provision to file an affidavit along with the application under Section 14 of the Act for taking physical possession.	The application filed by the bank under Section 14 of the Act for taking physical possession shall be accompanied by an affidavit duly affirmed by the authorised officer declaring the aggregate amount of dues, confirmation regarding the service of 13(2) notice on the borrower, disposal of objection raised by the borrower, etc. (Section 14[1]).

(Continued)

Table 3.2 (Continued)

Before the amendment of the SARFAESI Act	*After the amendment of the SARFAESI Act*
In case of the financing of a financial asset by more than one secured creditor or the joint financing of a financial asset, creditors representing *three-fourth* in value must agree to exercise the rights conferred under Section 13(4) of the Act.	In case of the financing of a financial asset by more than one secured creditor or joint financing of a financial asset, creditors representing *60%* in value must agree to exercise the rights conferred under Section 13(4) of the Act (Section 13[9]).
There was no provision empowering the district magistrate or the chief metropolitan magistrate to authorise any officer subordinate to him to take possession of the assets and documents under Section 14 of the Act.	The newly inserted Section 14(1A) of the Act empowers the district magistrate or the chief metropolitan magistrate to authorise any officer subordinate to him to take possession of the assets and documents under Section 14 of the Act (Section 14[1A]).
There was no provision to enable the securitisation and reconstruction company to file an application for the purpose of the substitution of its name in any pending suit, appeal or other proceedings.	The securitisation and reconstruction company may file application before the DRT or Appellate Tribunal for the purpose of the substitution of its name in any pending suit, appeal or other proceedings (Section 5[5]).
The Securitisation and Reconstruction of Financial Assets and Enforcement of Security Interest Act, 2002, did not allow securitisation or reconstruction companies to convert the debt of the borrower company into equity.	The Amendment Act provides for the conversion of any part of debt into shares of a borrower company (Section 9[g]).
The multi-state co-operative banks are not included in the definition of banks.	The multi-state co-operative banks are included in the definition of banks (Section 2[C][iv][a]).
There was no provision for the registration of transactions of securitisation, reconstruction or creation of a security interest in the Central Registry, which subsisted on or before the establishment of the Central Registry or to extend the time for filings of such transaction with the Central Registry.	The provision made for the registration of transactions of securitisation, reconstruction or creation of a security interest in the Central Registry, which subsisted on or before the establishment of Central Registry. It also gave powers to the central government to extend the time for filings of such transaction with the Central Registry (Section 26 A[1]).

(*Continued*)

Table 3.2 (Continued)

Before the amendment of the SARFAESI Act	*After the amendment of the SARFAESI Act*
There was no provision where the central government may exempt a class or classes of banks or financial institutions from the provisions of this Act on the grounds of public interest.	The central government may exempt a class or classes of banks or financial institutions from the provisions of this Act on the grounds of public interest (Section 31[A]).
There was no provision where the authorised officer shall serve, affix and publish notice of sale not less than 15 days to the borrower for any subsequent sale.	If the sale of movable or immovable property by any one of the methods specified by Sub-Rule (5) of Rule 8 fails and the sale is required to be conducted again, the authorised officer shall serve, affix and publish notice of sale not less than 15 days to the borrower for any subsequent sale (Rules 6[2] and 9[1]).
The secured assets shall not be transferred by way of lease, assignment or sale by the secured creditor where the dues of the secured creditor together with all costs, charges and expenses incurred by him are tendered to the secured creditor at any time before the date fixed for sale or transfer.	The secured assets shall not be transferred by way of lease, assignment or sale by the secured creditor where the dues of the secured creditor together with all costs, charges and expenses incurred by him are tendered to the secured creditor at any time before the date of publication of notice for public auction or inviting quotations or tender from public or private treaty for transfer by way of lease, assignment or sale of the secured assets (Section 13([8]).
There was no provision which accords priority over any subsequent security interest created upon secured property and any transfer by way of sale, lease or assignment or licence of such property or attachment order subsequent to such registration (Section 26[C]).	The claim of a secured creditor or other creditor holding an attachment order shall have priority over any subsequent security interest created upon such property, and any transfer by way of sale, lease or assignment or licence of such property or attachment order subsequent to such registration shall be subject to such claim (Section 26[C]).
There was no provision which provides priority to a secured creditor over all other debts and all revenues, taxes, cesses and other rates payable to the central government or state government or local authority.	Notwithstanding anything contained in any other law for the time being in force, after registration of security interest, debts due to any secured creditor shall be paid in priority over all other debts and all revenues, taxes, cesses and other rates payable to the central government or state government or local authority.

Table 3.3 Comparison of the provisions before and after the DRT Amendment Act.

Before the amendment of the DRT Act	*After the amendment if the DRT Act*
There was a provision which entitles a bank to file an application for the refund of the fees paid to the DRT if the bank settled the account at any stage of the proceedings before the final order was passed.	The banks can file an application for a refund of the fees paid to the DRT if the application is settled at any stage of the proceedings before the final order is passed (Section 19[3A] of the Act).
There was no provision wherein the defendant/borrower were bound to file a written statement within the stipulated period of time.	The defendant/borrower shall file a written statement within a period of 30 days from the date of service of the summons. If the defendant fails to file a written statement within the said period, the presiding officer may in exceptional cases allow not more than two extensions to the defendant to file a written statement (Section 19[5]).
There was no provision wherein the hearing of the application shall be completed within the stipulated period of time.	The hearing of the application shall be continued from day-to-day, and no adjournment shall be granted more than three times to a party, and where there are three or more parties, the total number of adjournments shall not exceed six (Section 19[5A]).
There was no provision wherein the presiding officer can impose a cost for granting an adjournment.	The presiding officer has been empowered to impose a cost for grant adjournments (Section 19[5A]).
The multi-state co-operative banks were not included in the definition of a bank in the Recovery of Debts Due to Banks and Financial Institutions Act, 1993.	The multi-state co-operative banks have been included in the definition of a bank in the Recovery of Debts Due to Banks and Financial Institutions Act, 1993 (Section 2[d][vi]).
There was no provision empowering the Debts Recovery Tribunal to pass an order acknowledging a settlement or compromise between the bank and borrower/guarantor.	In cases of a settlement or compromise between the bank and the borrower, the Debts Recovery Tribunal is empowered to pass an order acknowledging any such settlement or compromise (Section 19[20A]).

Conclusion

In the light of the previous discussion, it can be summarised that the constitutionality of the provisions of both the Recovery of Debts Due to Banks and Financial Institutions Act and the Securitisation and Reconstruction of Financial Assets and Enforcement of Security Interest Act have been upheld by the

Hon'ble Supreme, except for Section 17(2) of the SARFAESI Act, which was struck down by the Supreme Court as arbitrary and unconstitutional.

* * * * * * * * * * * * * * *

Notes

1 Delhi High Court Bar Association and Another v. Union of India and Others reported in AIR 1995 Delhi 323.
2 Assam Leather Industry v. Union of India (UOI) and Others on August 16, 1999: 2001 104 CompCas 115 Gauhati/Indian Kanoon – http://indiankanoon.org/doc/1237648/.
3 K. Abdul Khader and Others v. Union of India and Others reported in AIR 2001 Kant 179.
4 Union of India and Another v. Delhi High Court Bar Association and Others reported in AIR 2002 SC 1479, 2002(2) SCR 450, (2002) 4 SCC 275.
5 D.K. Abdul Khader and Others v. Union of India and Others reported in AIR 2001 Kant 179.
6 Allahabad Bank v. Canara Bank and Another, AIR 2000 SC 1535, (2000) 4 SCC 406.
7 Punjab National Bank, Dasuya v. Chajju Ram and Others, AIR 2000 SC 2671.
8 "A comparative study of non-performing assets in India in the global context – similarities and dissimilarities, remedial measures" – paper by Shri. Prashanth K. Reddy, The Indian Institute of Management Ahmedabad, India.
9 *The Financial Stability Report*, Issue No. 9, by the Reserve Bank of India, June 2014.
10 https://www.livemint.com (accessed on January 2, 2024).
11 Mardia Chemicals Ltd v. Union of India, AIR 2004 SC 2371.
12 Keshavlal Khemchand and Sons Pvt. Ltd v. Union of India and Others, Writ Petition (Civil) No.901 of 2014.
13 M/s. Decan Chronicles Holdings Limited v. Union of India and Others, W.P.No.5897/2014.
14 RBI Mater Circular no. DBOD.No.BP.BC.9/21.04.048/2014–15 dated July 1, 2014.
15 ITO v. Mohd Kunhi, (1969) 2 SCR 65.
16 Allahabad Bank v. Radha Krishna Maity, (1999) 6 SCC 755.
17 M/s. Mercury Exporters and Manufacturing Pvt. Ltd & Another v. Punjab National Bank and Another, W.P.No.353 of 2014.
18 Ganga Bai v. Vijay Kumar, (1974) 2 SCC 393
19 Mardia Chemicals Ltd v. Union of India, AIR 2004 SC 2371.
20 Mardia Chemicals Ltd v. Union of India, AIR 2004 SC 2371.
21 Ramaswamy Aiyengar v. Kailasa Thevar, 1951 SCR 292.
22 Dahya Lal v. Rasul Mohd. Abdul Rahim, (1963) 3 SCR.
23 Kanshi Ram v. Lachhman, (2001) 5 SCC 546.
24 L. Chandrakumar v. Union of India, (1997) 3 SCC 261.
25 Surya Dev Rai v. Ram Chander Rai, (2003) 6 SCC 675.
26 Mardia Chemicals Ltd v. Union of India, AIR 2004 SC 2371.
27 Mardia Chemicals v. Union of India, (2004) 4 SCC 311.
28 V. Narasimhachariar v. Egmore Benefit Society, 3rd Branch Ltd., AIR 1955 Mad. 135, V.P.; Padmavati v. P.S. Swaminathan Iyer, AIR 1955 Mad. 343 (sic).
29 Bank of Maharashtra Ltd v. Official Liquidator, High Court Buildings, AIR 1969 Mys. 280.

Chapter 4

Legislations relating to the recovery of dues to banks in force in India

The extending of credit facilities for economic activities is the main raison d'être of banking. Apart from raising resources through fresh deposits, borrowings, etc., the recycling of funds received back from borrowers constitutes a major part of funding credit dispensation activity. Non-recovery of instalments as interest on the loan portfolio negates the effectiveness of this process of a credit cycle. Non-recovery also affects the profitability of banks and requires them to maintain more owned funds by way of capital and the creation of reserves and provisions to act as cushion for the loan losses. Avoidance of loan losses in the business of banking may not be possible, and the attempts of bank managements shall be to keep the losses at a low level. In fact, it is the level of non-performing assets which primarily differentiates between good and bad banks. Mounting level of non-performing assets (NPAs) have widespread repercussions in the economy.

In India, the non-performing assets (NPA), which are at higher levels than those in other countries, have lately attracted the attention of the public as well as of international financial institutions. This gained further prominence in the wake of transparency and disclosure measures initiated by the Reserve Bank of India in recent years. The various committees set up by the Reserve Bank of India and Ministry of Finance in the Government of India have studied the alarming rise of non-performing assets and submitted their reports on taking further action to end the menace of non-performing assets.

The Reserve Bank of India has constituted a study group under the supervision of Shri. A.Q. Siddiqi, Chief General Manager, Department of Banking Supervision, to study the recovery procedures adopted by the bank for the recovery of non-performing assets in banks.[1] The study group studied data from 33 banks (27 public sectors and 6 private sectors), and the study of the files relating to the measures taken for recovery by way of suits filed by the 15 banks revealed that banks do file suits, exhausting other means of recovery. During 1996, the suits filed accounted for 26.21% of these banks' NPAs. In 1997 and 1998 this was further increased to 33.91% and 46.38% respectively. The recoveries made from suits filed by these 33 banks during the 3 years (from 1996 to 1998) were 7.33%, 4.74% and 4.32%

DOI: 10.4324/9781003546238-4

respectively, which is evidence of a decreasing trend of recovery through this route. In view of such a meagre recovery, before filing suit the banks weigh the likely recovery prospects and the opportunity cost of any amounts that could be recovered immediately. Suit filing, as such, is resorted to as the last alternative.

I. The Recovery of Debts and Bankruptcy Act, 1993 (RDB Act)

The Recovery of Debts Due to Banks and Financial Institutions Act (RDDBFI Act) was enacted for the establishment of tribunals for expeditious adjudication and the recovery of debts due to banks and financial institutions and for matters connected therewith or incidental thereto. The Recovery of Debts Due to Banks and Financial Institutions Bill was passed by both Houses of Parliament and received the assent of the president on 27th August 1993. It went on the Statute Book as The Recovery of Debts Due to Banks and Financial Institutions Act, 1993 (51 of 1993). The name of the Recovery of Debts Due to Banks and Financial Institutions and Bankruptcy Act was renamed as the Recovery of Debts and Bankruptcy Act, 1993 vide the Amendment Act, 30 of 2016 (hereinafter referred to as RDB Act). The provisions of this Act shall not apply where the amount of debt due to any bank or financial institution or to a consortium of banks or financial institutions is less than 10 lakh rupees or such other amount, being not less than 1 lakh rupee, as the Central Government may, by notification, specify. Later on, the Ministry of Finance vide notification dated 6th September, 2018 has increased the pecuniary jurisdiction of Tribunals from Rs.10 lakhs to Rs.20 lakhs.

1. The definition of the term "Debt"

The section 2(g) of the RDB Act defines the term "debt". Debt means any liability (inclusive of interest) which is claimed as due from any person by a bank or a financial institution or by a consortium of banks or financial institutions during the course of any business activity undertaken by the bank or the financial institution or the consortium under any law for the time being in force, in cash or otherwise, whether secured or unsecured, or assigned, or whether payable under a decree or order of any civil court or any arbitration award or otherwise or under a mortgage and subsisting on, and legally recoverable on the date of the application. This definition of debt is of high importance because in many cases, the borrowers and guarantors have challenged the claim of the banks as not falling within the definition.

2. The jurisdiction, powers and authority of tribunals

Another important provision is Section 17. This section defines the jurisdiction, powers and authority of tribunals. In terms of this provision, the

Tribunal shall exercise, on and from the appointed day, the jurisdiction, powers and authority to entertain and decide applications from the banks and financial institutions for the recovery of debts due to such banks and financial institutions. The Section 17(A) of the Act defined the powers of the Appellate Tribunal. The Appellate Tribunal shall exercise, on and from the appointed day, the jurisdiction, powers and authority to entertain appeals against any order made, or deemed to have been made, by a tribunal under this Act.

The Section 18 of the RDBI Act bars the jurisdiction of other courts from entertaining matters pertaining to the recovery of dues of banks. It states that on and from the appointed day, no court or other authority shall have, or be entitled to exercise, any jurisdiction, power or authority (except the Supreme Court or a High Court exercising jurisdiction under Articles 226 and 227 of the Constitution) in relation to the matters specified in Section 17.

3. *The procedure for filing application*

The Section 19 of the RDB Act deals with the modus operandi for the filing of application by banks for the recovery of dues. It states that

(1) Where a bank or a financial institution has to recover any debt from any person, it may make an application to the Tribunal within the local limits of whose jurisdiction

  (a) the defendant, or each of the defendants where there are more than one, at the time of making the application, actually and voluntarily resides or carries on business or personally works for gain; or
  (b) any of the defendants, where there are more than one, at the time of making the application, actually and voluntarily resides or carries on business or personally works for gain; or
  (c) the cause of action, wholly or in party, arises.

(2) Where a bank or a financial institution, which has to recover its debt from any person, has filed an application to the Tribunal under Sub-Section (1) and against the same person another bank or financial institution also has claim to recover its debt, then, the later bank or financial institution may join the applicant bank or financial institution at any stage of the proceedings, before the final order is passed, by making an application to that tribunal.
(3) Every application under Sub-Section (1) or Sub-Section (2) shall be in such form and accompanied by such documents or other evidence and by such fee as may be prescribed:
(4) On receipt of the application under Sub-Section (1) or Sub-Section (2), the Tribunal shall issue summons requiring the defendant to show cause within 30 days of the service of summons as to why the relief prayed for should not be granted.
(5) The defendant shall, at or before the first hearing or within such time as the Tribunal may permit, present a written statement in his defence.

(6) Where the defendant claims to set-off against the applicant's demand any ascertained sum of money legally recoverable by him from such applicant, the defendant may, at the first hearing of the application, but not afterwards unless permitted by the Tribunal, present a written statement containing the particulars of the debt sought to be set-off.

(7) The written statement shall have the same effect as a plaint in a cross-suit so as to enable the Tribunal to pass a final order in respect both of the original claim and of the set-off.

(8) A defendant in an application may, in addition to his right of pleading a set-off under Sub-Section (6), set up, by way of counter-claim against the claim of the applicant, any right or claim in respect of a cause of action accruing to the defendant against the applicant either before or after the filing of the application but before the defendant has delivered his defence or before the time limited for delivering his defence has expired, whether such counter-claim is in the nature of a claim for damages or not.

(9) A counter-claim under Sub-Section (8) shall have the same effect as a cross-suit so as to enable the Tribunal to pass a final order on the same application, both on the original claim and on the counter-claim.

(10) The applicant shall be at liberty to file a written statement in answer to the counter-claim of the defendant within such period as may be fixed by the Tribunal.

(11) Where a defendant sets up a counter-claim and the applicant contends that the claim thereby raised ought not be disposed of by way of counter-claim but in an independent action, the applicant may, at any time before issues are settled in relation to the counter-claim, apply to the Tribunal for an order that such counter-claim may be excluded, and the Tribunal may, on the hearing of such application, make such order as it thinks fit.

4. *The powers of the Tribunal to pass interim orders*

Section 19(12) of the RDB Act dealt with the powers of the Tribunal to pass interim orders. It empowered the Tribunal to pass interim order (whether by way of injunction or stay or attachment) against the defendant to debar him from transferring, alienating or otherwise dealing with, or disposing of, any property and assets belonging to him without the prior permission of the Tribunal.

Section 19 (13) (A) further states that where, at any stage of the proceedings, the Tribunal is satisfied, by affidavit or otherwise, that the defendant, with intent to obstruct or delay or frustrate the execution of any order for the recovery of debt that may be passed against him,

(1) is about to dispose of the whole or any part of his property; or

(2) is about to remove the whole or any part of his property from the local limits of the jurisdiction of the Tribunal; or

(3) is likely to cause any damage or mischief to the property or affect its value by misuse or creating third party interest,

the Tribunal may direct the defendant, within a time to be fixed by it, either to furnish security, in such sum as may be specified in the order, to produce and place at the disposal of the Tribunal, when required, the said property or the value of the same, or such portion thereof as may be sufficient to satisfy the certificate for the recovery of the debt, or to appear and show cause why he should not furnish security.

Section 19 (13) (B) states that where the defendant fails to show cause as to why he should not furnish security, or fails to furnish the security required, within the time fixed by the Tribunal, the Tribunal may order the attachment of the whole or such portion of the properties claimed by the applicant as the properties secured in his favour or otherwise owned by the defendant as appears sufficient to satisfy any certificate for the recovery of debt.

The Tribunal may also in the order direct the conditional attachment of the whole or any portion of the property specified under sub-section. If an order of attachment is made without complying with the provisions of Sub-Section 13, such attachment shall be void. In the case of disobedience of an order made by the Tribunal or breach of any of the terms on which the order was made, the Tribunal may order the properties of the person guilty of such disobedience or breach to be attached and may also order such person to be detained in the civil prison for a term not exceeding three months, unless in the meantime the Tribunal directs his release.

5. *The powers of the Tribunal to appoint receivers*

The powers of the Tribunal to appoint receivers are given in Section 19(18). It states that where it appears to the Tribunal to be just and convenient, the Tribunal may, by order

(1) Appoint a receiver of any property, whether before or after grant of certificate for recovery of debt;
(2) Remove any person from the possession or custody of the property;
(3) Commit the same to the possession, custody or management of the receiver;
(4) Confer upon the receiver all such powers, as to bringing and defending suits in the courts or filing and defending application before the Tribunal and for the realisation, management, protection, preservation and improvement of the property; the collection of the rents and profits thereof; the application and disposal of such rents and profits; and the execution of documents as the owner himself has, or such of those powers as the Tribunal thinks fit; and appoint a commissioner for the preparation of an inventory of the properties of the defendant or for the sale thereof.

6. *Issue of debt certificate by the Tribunal*

The other relevant provisions under S.19 that deal with the issue of a certificate by the Tribunal are cited as follows:

(19) Where a certificate of recovery is issued against a company as defined under the Companies Act, 2013 (18 of 2013) and such company is under liquidation, the Tribunal may by an order direct that the sale proceeds of secured assets of such company be distributed in the same manner as provided in section 326 of the Companies Act, 2013 or under any other law for the time being in force.

(20) The Tribunal may, after giving the applicant and the defendant, an opportunity of being heard, in respect of all claims, set-off or counter-claim, if any, and interest on such claims, within thirty days from the date of conclusion of the hearings, pass interim or final order as it deems fit which may include order for payment of interest from the date on which payment of the amount is found due up to the date of realisation or actual payment.

(20A) Where it is proved to the satisfaction of the Tribunal that the claim of the applicant has been adjusted wholly or in part by any lawful agreement or compromise in writing and signed by the parties or where the defendant has repaid or agreed to repay the claim of the applicant, the Tribunal shall pass orders recording such agreement, compromise or satisfaction of the claim.

(20AA) While passing the final order under sub-section (20), the Tribunal shall clearly specify the assets of the borrower which security interest is created in favour of any bank or financial institution and direct the Recovery Officers to distribute the sale proceeds of such assets as provided in sub-section (20AB).

(20AB) Notwithstanding anything to the contrary contained in any law for the time being in force, the proceeds from sale of secured assets shall be distributed in the following orders of priority, namely:— (i) the costs incurred for preservation and protection of secured assets, the costs of valuation, public notice for possession and auction and other expenses for sale of assets shall be paid in full; (ii) debts owed to the bank or financial institution. Explanation.—For the purposes of this sub-section, it is hereby clarified that on or after the commencement of the Insolvency and Bankruptcy Code, 2016 (31 of 2016), in cases where insolvency and bankruptcy proceedings are pending in respect of secured assets of the borrower, the distribution of proceeds from the sale of secured assets shall be subject to the order of priority as provided in that Code.

(21) (i) The Tribunal shall send a copy of its final order and the recovery certificate, to the applicant and defendant. (ii) The applicant and the defendant may obtain copy of any order passed by the Tribunal on payment on such fee as may be prescribed.

(22) The Presiding Officer shall issue a certificate of recovery along with the final order, under sub-section (20), for payment of debt with interest under his signature to the Recovery Officer for recovery of the amount of debt specified in the certificate.

(22A) Any recovery certificate issued by the Presiding Officer under sub-section (22) shall be deemed to be decree or order of the Court for the purposes of initiation of winding up proceedings against a company registered under the Companies Act, 2013 (18 of 2013) or Limited Liability Partnership registered under the Limited Liability Partnership Act, 2008 (6 of 2009) or insolvency proceedings against any individual or partnership firm under any law for the time being in force, as the case may be.

(23) Where the Tribunal, which has issued a certificate of recovery, is satisfied that the property is situated within the local limits of the jurisdiction of two or more Tribunals, it may send the copies of the certificate of recovery for execution to such other Tribunals where the property is situated: Provided that in a case where the Tribunal to which the certificate of recovery is sent for execution finds that it has no jurisdiction to comply with the certificate of recovery, it shall return the same to the Tribunal which has issued it.

(24) The application made to the Tribunal under sub-section (1) or sub-section (2) shall be dealt with by it as expeditiously as possible and 1[every effort shall be made by it to complete the proceedings in two hearings, and] to dispose of the application finally within one hundred and eighty days from the date of receipt of the application.

(25) The Tribunal may made such orders and give such directions as may be necessary or expedient to give effect to its orders or to prevent abuse of its process or to secure the ends of justice.

7. *The filing of an appeal before DRAT*

Section 20 of the RDB Act deals with filing an appeal before DRAT. It says that any person aggrieved by an order made, or deemed to have been made, by a tribunal under this Act, may prefer an appeal to an Appellate Tribunal having jurisdiction in the matter.

Section 20 (2) No appeal shall lie to the Appellate Tribunal from an order made by a Tribunal with the consent of the parties.

Section 20 (2) Every appeal under Sub-Section (1) shall be filed within a period of 30 days from the date on which a copy of the order made, or deemed to have been made, by the Tribunal is received by him and it shall be in such form and be accompanied by such fee as may be prescribed:

Provided that the Appellate Tribunal may entertain an appeal after the expiry of the said period of 45 days if it is satisfied that there was sufficient cause for not filing it within that period.

Section 20 (4) On receipt of an appeal under Sub-Section (1) or under Section 181(1) of the Insolvency and Bankruptcy Code, 2016, the Appellate Tribunal may, after giving the parties to the appeal, an opportunity of being heard, pass such orders thereon as it thinks fit, confirming, modifying or setting aside the order appealed against.

Section 20 (6) of the RDB Act stipulates that the appeal filed before the Appellate Tribunal under Sub-Section (1) shall be dealt with as expeditiously as possible and endeavours shall be made to dispose of the appeal within 6 months from the date of the receipt of the appeal.

8. The deposit of an amount of debt on filing an appeal

Section 21 of the RDB Act stipulates the deposit of an amount of debt on filing an appeal. It states that where an appeal is preferred by any person from whom the amount of debt is due to a bank or a financial institution or a consortium of banks or financial institutions, such appeal shall not be entertained by the Appellate Tribunal unless such person has deposited with the Appellate Tribunal 50% of the amount of debt due from him as determined by the Tribunal under Section 19. The Section further states that the Appellate Tribunal may, for reasons to be recorded in writing, reduce the amount to be deposited upto 25% of the amount due.

9. The Tribunal shall be guided by the principles of natural justice

Section 22 of the RDB Act deals with the procedure and powers of the Tribunal and the Appellate Tribunal. It states that the Tribunal and the Appellate Tribunal shall not be bound by the procedure laid down by the Code of Civil Procedure, 1908 (5 of 1908), but it shall be guided by the principles of natural justice and, subject to the other provisions of this Act and of any rules, the Tribunal and the Appellate Tribunal shall have powers to regulate their own procedure including the places at which they shall have their sittings.

10. The Tribunal shall have powers of civil court

The Tribunal and the Appellate Tribunal shall have, for the purposes of discharging their functions under this Act, the same powers as are vested in a civil court under the Code of Civil Procedure, 1908 (5 of 1908), while trying a suit, in respect of the following matters, namely

(1) Summoning and enforcing the attendance of any person and examining him on oath;
(2) Requiring the discovery and production of documents;
(3) Receiving evidence on affidavits;
(4) Issuing commissions for the examination of witnesses or documents;
(5) Reviewing its decisions;
(6) Dismissing an application for default or deciding it *ex parte*;
(7) Setting aside any order of dismissal of any application for default or any order passed by it *ex parte*;
(8) Any other matter which may be prescribed.

11. Modes of recovery

Section 25 of the RDB Act deals with the modes of the recovery of debts. The recovery officer shall, on receipt of the copy of the certificate under Sub-Section (7) of Section 19, proceed to recover the amount of debt specified in the certificate by one or more of the following modes, namely

(a) Attachment and sale of the movable or immovable property of the defendant;
(aa) Taking possession of property over which security interest is created or any other property of the defendant and appointing receiver for such property and to sell the same;
(b) Arrest of the defendant and his detention in prison;
(c) Appointing a receiver for the management of the movable or immovable properties of the defendant;
(d) Any other mode of recovery as may be prescribed by the Central Government.

Section 27 of the RDB Act deals with the stay of proceedings under certificate and amendment or withdrawal thereof. It states that notwithstanding that a certificate has been issued to the recovery officer for the recovery of any amount, the presiding officer may grant time for the payment of the amount, provided the defendant makes a down payment of not less than 25% of the amount specified in the recovery certificate and gives an unconditional undertaking to pay the balance within a rcasonablc timc, which is acceptable to the applicant bank or financial institutions holding recovery certificate.

Where a certificate for the recovery of amount has been issued, the presiding officer shall keep the recovery officer informed of any amount paid or time granted for payment, subsequent to the issue of such certificate to the recovery officer.

Where the order giving rise to a demand of amount for recovery of debt has been modified in appeal, and, as a consequence thereof the demand is reduced, the presiding officer shall stay the recovery of such part of the amount of the certificate as pertains to the said reduction for the period for which the appeal remains pending.

Where a certificate for the recovery of debt has been received by the recovery officer and subsequently the amount of the outstanding demands is reduced (or enhanced) as a result of an appeal, the presiding officer shall, when the order which was the subject matter of such appeal has become final and conclusive, amend the certificate or withdraw it, as the case may be.

12. Other modes of recovery

Section 28 deals with other modes of recovery. Where a certificate has been issued to the recovery officer under Sub-Section (7) of Section 19, the recovery officer may, without prejudice to the modes of recovery specified in Section 25, recover the amount of debt by any one or more of the modes provided under section 28 of the Act.

28(2) If any amount is due from any person to the defendant, the recovery officer may require such person to deduct from the said amount, the amount of debt due from the defendant under this Act and such person shall comply with any such requisition and shall pay the sum so deducted to the credit of the recovery officer:

28(3) (i) The recovery officer may, at any time or from time to time, by notice in writing, require any person from whom money is due or may become due to the defendant or to any person who holds or may subsequently hold money for or on account of the defendant, to pay to the recovery officer either forthwith upon the money becoming due or being held or within the time specified in the notice (not being before the money becomes due or is held) so much of the money as is sufficient to pay the amount of debt due from the defendant or the whole of the money when it is equal to or less than that amount.

(ii) A notice under this sub-section may be issued to any person who holds or may subsequently hold any money for or on account of the defendant jointly with any other person and for the purposes of this sub-section, the shares of the joint holders in such amount shall be presumed, until the contrary is proved, to be equal.

(iii) A copy of the notice shall be forwarded to the defendant at his last address known to the recovery officer and in the case of a joint account to all the joint holders at their last addresses known to the recovery officer.

(iv) Save as otherwise provided in this sub-section, every person to whom a notice is issued under the sub-section shall be bound to comply with such notice, and, in particular, where any such notice is issued to a post office, bank, financial institution, or an insurer, it shall not be necessary for any pass book, deposit receipt, policy or any other document to be produced for the purpose of any entry, endorsement or the like to be made before the payment is made notwithstanding any rule, practice or requirement to the contrary.

(v) Any claim respecting any property in relation to which a notice under this sub-section has been issued arising after the date of the notice shall be void as against any demand contained in the notice.

(vi) Where a person to whom a notice under this sub-section is sent objects to it by a statement on oath that the sum demanded or the part thereof is not due to the defendant or that he does not hold any money for or on account of the defendant, then, nothing contained in this sub-section shall be deemed to require such person to pay any such sum or part thereof, as the case may be, but if it is discovered that such statement was false in any material particular, such person shall be personally liable to the recovery officer to the extent of his own liability to the defendant on the date of the notice, or to the extent of the defendant's liability for any sum due under this Act, whichever is less.

(vii) The recovery officer may, at any time or from time to time, amend or revoke any notice under this sub-section or extend the time for making any payment in pursuance of such notice.

(viii) The recovery officer shall grant a receipt for any amount paid in compliance with a notice issued under this sub-section, and the person so paying shall be fully discharged from his liability to the defendant to the extent of the amount so paid.

(ix) Any person discharging any liability to the defendant after the receipt of a notice under this sub-section shall be personally liable to the recovery officer to the extent of his own liability to the defendant so discharged or to the extent of the defendant's liability for any debt due under this Act, whichever is less.

(x) If the person to whom a notice under this sub-section is sent fails to make payment in pursuance thereof to the recovery officer, he shall be deemed to be a defendant in default in respect of the amount specified in the notice and further proceedings may be taken against him for the realisation of the amount as if it were a debt due from him, in the manner provided in Sections 25, 26 and 27, and the notice shall have the same effect as an attachment of a debt by the recovery officer in exercise of his powers under Section 25.

28(4) The recovery officer may apply to the court in whose custody there is money belonging to the defendant for payment to him of the entire amount of such money, or if it is more than the amount of debt due an amount sufficient to discharge the amount of debt so due.

28(4) (A) The recovery officer may, by order, at any stage of the execution of the certificate of recovery, require any person, and in case of a company, any of its officers against whom or which the certificate of recovery is issued, to declare on affidavit the particulars of his or its assets.

28(5) The recovery officer may recover any amount of debt due from the defendant by distraint and sale of his movable property in the manner laid down in the Third Schedule to the Income-Tax Act, 1961 (43 of 1961).

13. *Application of the provisions of the Income-tax Act*

The Section 29 deals with the application of certain provisions of the Income-tax Act to the RDB Act. The provisions of the Second and Third Schedules to the Income-tax Act, 1961, and the Income-tax (Certificate Proceedings) Rules, 1962, as in force from time to time shall, as far as possible, apply with necessary modifications as if the said provisions and the rules referred to the amount of debt due under this Act instead of to the Income-tax: provided that any reference under the said provisions and the rules to the "assessee" shall be construed as a reference to the defendant under this Act.

The Section 30 deals with an appeal against the order of the recovery officer. Notwithstanding anything contained in Section 29, any person aggrieved by an order of the recovery officer made under this Act may, within 30 days from the date on which a copy of the order is issued to him, prefer an appeal to the Tribunal. On receipt of an appeal under Sub-Section (1) the Tribunal may, after giving an opportunity to the appellant to be heard and after making such inquiry as it deems fit, confirm, modify or set aside the order made by the recovery officer in exercise of his powers under Sections 25 to 28 (both inclusive).

14. *Transfer of pending cases*

The Section 31 of the Act deals with the transfer of pending cases. Every suit or other proceeding pending before any court immediately before the date of establishment of a tribunal under this Act, being a suit or proceeding the cause of action whereon it is based is such that it would have been, if it had arisen after such establishment, within the jurisdiction of such tribunal, stood transferred on that date to such tribunal provided that nothing in this sub-section applied to any appeal pending as aforesaid before any court.

The section 31(2) state that where any suit or other proceeding stands transferred from any court to a Tribunal under Sub-Section (1)

(a) The court shall, as soon as may be after such transfer, forward the records of such suit or other proceeding to the Tribunal; and
(b) The Tribunal may, on receipt of such records, proceed to deal with such suit or other proceeding, so far as may be, in the same manner as in the case of an application made under Section 19 from the stage which was reached before such transfer or from any earlier stage as the Tribunal may deem fit.

The Section 34 of the Act state that the RDB Act will have an overriding effect. Save as provided under Sub-Section (2), the provisions of this Act shall have effect notwithstanding anything inconsistent therewith contained in any other law for the time being in force or in any instrument having effect by virtue of any law other than this Act.

II. The Securitisation and Reconstruction of Financial Assets and Enforcement of Security Interest Act, 2002 (SARFAESI Act)

The Securitisation and Reconstruction of Financial Assets and Enforcement of Security Interest Act, 2002, was enacted with an intention to strengthen the creditors' rights through enforcement of securities by the banks and financial institutions by conferring on the creditors the right to seize and sell the secured asset in order to recover dues promptly, bypassing the costly and very time-consuming legal court process.

The Securitisation and Reconstruction of Financial Assets and Enforcement of Security Interest Act (hereinafter referred to as SARFEASI Act) basically deals with five aspects:

(1) Enforcement of security interest by secured creditor – banks/financial institutions.
(2) Transfer of non-performing assets to an asset reconstruction company.
(3) Provide a legal framework for securitisation of assets.
(4) Enforce the secured assets for recovery of dues to the bank.
(5) Provide for adjudication of grievances of the affected persons.

Looking from the standpoint of practicality, in essence, the SARFEASI Act has four different dimensions which are displayed in Figure 4.1.

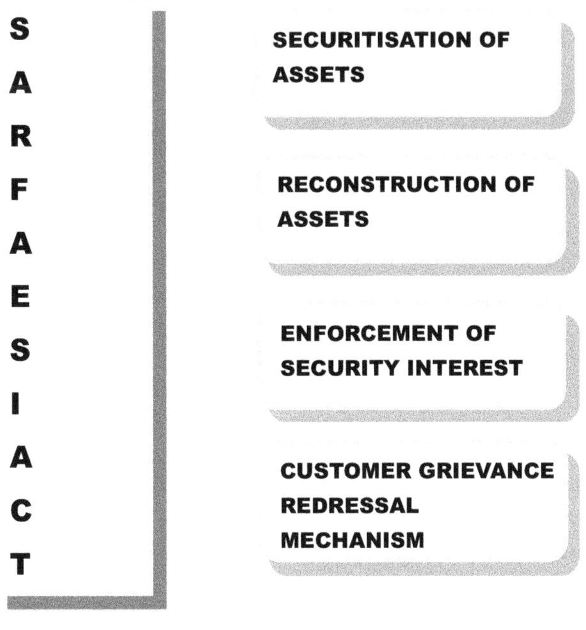

Figure 4.1 Pictorial representation of the four dimensions of the SARFAESI Act

It is important to note that since the proceedings under the SARFAESI Act are non-judicial and non-adjudicatory procedures, the authorised officer must ensure that the provisions of the SARFAESI Act and Rules are strictly complied with in their true spirit. The Hon'ble Supreme Court of India in its judgement[2] upheld that banks can take action against the defaulting borrower under the SARFAESI Act and also simultaneously proceed against the same borrower at DRT. The Hon'ble Court observed that the SARFAESI Act is an additional remedy and is not inconsistent with the DRT Act.[3] We may examine the provisions of the SARFAESI Act and Rules in detail so as to understand whether the principles of natural justice and other canons of jurisprudence have been applied in this Act.

1. Service of notice

In order to ensure the principles of natural justice are being complied with, the SARFAESI Act contains stringent provisions regarding the serving of notice to the borrower/guarantor before initiating SARFAESI proceedings for taking possession of secured assets. The initiation of proceedings under the SARFAESI Act starts with issuing a demand notice under Section 13(2) of the Act. The rights of the secured creditor under this Act may be exercised by one or more his officers authorised in this behalf in such manner as may be prescribed. According to the rules, the authorised officer who can take action under this Act shall be an officer not less than a chief manager (officer in the scale of Senior Management Cadre IV) of the public sector banks or equivalent as specified by the Board of Directors or Board of Trustees of the secured creditor. The service of 13(2) Demand Notices needs to be made by delivering or transmitting at the place where the borrower, or his agent empowered to accept the notice or documents on behalf of the borrower, actually and voluntarily resides or carried on business or personally works for gain, by registered post with acknowledgement due addressed to the borrower or his agent or by speed post or courier or any means of transmission of documents like fax message or electronic mail service.

The demand notice under Secion 13(2) of the Act shall give details of the amount payable by the borrower and the secured assets intended to be enforced by the secured creditor in the event of non-payment of secured debts by the borrower/guarantor. The date on which the account was classified as a non-performing asset shall also be specifically mentioned in the 13(2) notice. The particulars of complete loan documents executed by the borrower, i.e. term loan agreement, cash credit agreement, supplementary documents and revival letters, balance confirmation letters, deposit of title deeds confirmation letter, etc., should be stated very clearly in the schedule of notice. In a case where a 13(2) Demand Notice is issued against both mortgaged and hypothecated properties, separate schedules must be provided each for mortgaged and hypothecated property.

In order to bring more transparency, the Government of India's Ministry of Finance has told all banks/financial institutions that while issuing a Demand Notice under Section 13(2) of the SARFAESI Act, the banks should attach a statement of account from the date of declaration of NPA up to the date of the demand notice clearly indicating the rate of interest charged.

2. *Non-service of notice*

If demand notices could not be served on the borrower(s)/guarantor(s), then as per the SARFAESI Rules, the service should be effected by affixing a copy of the Demand Notice on the outer door/other conspicuous place where the borrower(s)/guarantor(s) reside, and the contents of the notice should be published in two leading newspapers, one in vernacular, having sufficient circulation in that locality.

3. *Reply to representation or objection*

Upon receipt of the notice, if the borrower/guarantor makes any representation or raises any objection, the secured creditor (bank) shall consider such representation or objection, and if the secured creditor (bank) comes to the conclusion that such representation or objection is not acceptable or tenable, the secured creditor/bank shall communicate, within 15 days of receipt of such representation or objection, the reasons for non-acceptance of the representation or objection to the borrower/guarantor. In order to ensure the application of the legal maxim "no one should be a judge in his own case, many of the public sector banks have issued internal circulars stating that the objections should be considered by an authority higher than the notice issuing authority".

4. *Limitation period*

It is pertinent to note that exercising the powers under this Act does not save the period of limitation. The authorised officer of bank cannot exercise the rights under this Act in respect of time-barred debts. With respect to consortium lending accounts, wherein the security is shared by more than one bank/financial institution, consent from all other secured creditors should necessarily be sought before the issue of notice. Thereafter, if at least 60% of the secured creditors by value agree, the bank that is leading the consortium lending should initiate action under this Act.

5. *Further proceedings after expiry of 60 days in the Section 13(2) notice*

Where there is no response from the borrower against the notice issued under Section 13(2) of the SARFAESI Act, the authorised officer of bank may take the following steps:

(1) After expiry of the 60-day notice period and the borrower(s)/guarantor(s) failed to discharge the debt, possession notice under Section 13(4) is

required to be served, and steps may be taken to take possession of the secured asset.

(2) Where the mortgaged property is let-out or information of receivables due to the borrower/guarantor are known, notice may be served on tenants/sundry debtors to pay the amounts due and payable to the borrower/guarantor to the bank instead.

(3) Any payment made by any person to the secured creditor (bank) shall give such person a valid discharge as if he has made payment to the borrower.

III. Taking possession of movable assets

As discussed earlier, after expiry of the 60-day notice, if the borrower(s)/guarantor(s) failed to discharge the debt, the authorised officer shall take possession of such movable property in the presence of two witnesses after panchanama is drawn and duly signed by the witnesses.

The authorised officer may file the necessary application/petition before the chief metropolitan magistrate or district magistrate within whose jurisdiction the secured assets/documents are situated or found for obtaining orders for eviction. The application filed by the bank under Section 14 of the Act for taking physical possession shall be accompanied by an affidavit duly affirmed by the authorised officer declaring the aggregate amount of dues, confirmation regarding the service of the 13(2) notice on the borrower, disposal of objection raised by the borrower, etc. (Section 14[1]).

It is important to note that no act of the chief metropolitan magistrate or the district magistrate done under the SARFAESI Act shall be called in question in any court or before any authority under Section 14(3) of the Act.

After taking possession, the authorised officer should make an inventory of the property and deliver a copy of such inventory to the borrower/guarantor or any person authorised to receive it on their behalf.

The property under possession should be kept in the custody of the authorised officer or in the custody of any person authorised or appointed by him. The authorised officer or his custodian should take as much care of the property as a man of ordinary prudence would, under similar circumstances, take of his own property.

If the property taken possession of is subject to a speedy and natural decay, or the expenses of keeping such property in custody are likely to exceed its value, the authorised officer may sell it at once.

1. Taking possession of immovable assets

The authorised officer shall take possession of the immovable property by issuing a possession notice as per the format given in the rules. The following step needs to be undertaken by the authorised officer/branch officials:

- As per the amendment made in Rule 8(2) of the Security Interest (enforcement) rules,[4] the possession notice shall also be published, as soon as possible, but in any case, not later than 7 days from the date of taking possession in two leading newspapers, one in vernacular language that has sufficient circulation in that locality.

In order to take actual physical possession or control of secured assets, the authorised officer may file necessary an application/petition before the chief metropolitan magistrate or the district magistrate within whose jurisdiction the secured assets/documents are situated or found. The application filed by the bank under Section 14 of the Act for taking physical possession shall be accompanied by an affidavit duly affirmed by the authorised officer declaring the aggregate amount of dues, confirmation regarding the service of the 13(2) notice to the borrower, disposal of objection raised by the borrower, etc. (Section 14[1]). At this point, the Bank branches may engage the service of their panel advocates. The chief metropolitan magistrate or the district magistrate, on request of the authorised officer, may issue necessary orders for assistance to take possession of such assets and documents relating thereto and forward such assets and documents to the secured creditor.

2. *Valuation of the movable and immovable assets*

In order to ensure that the properties taken possession by banks/FIs through an authorised officer are sold at a fair price, the provisions have been incorporated in the SARFAESI Act for obtaining a valuation report from the valuer whose name has been approved by the board of directors of the bank and is registered as valuer under the provisions of the Wealth Tax Act. Hence, immediately after taking possession and before the sale, the authorised officer should arrange for a valuation of the assets by an approved valuer.

As per the amendment made in Rule 2(d) of the Security Interest (Enforcement) Rules, 2002, an approved valuer means a person registered as a valuer under Section 34(AB) of the Wealth Tax Act, 1957 and approved by the board of directors or the board of trustees of the secured creditor.

As per the practice prevailing in banks/FIs, the reserve price is approved by a committee consisting of senior officials. The reserve price of the assets to be sold may be determined on the basis of the valuation obtained. The committee will approve the reserve price and convey the same to the authorised officer. No sale should be finalised below the reserve price fixed by the SARFAESI valuation committee. If it is found that the reserve price cannot be realised, the authorised officer may submit fresh recommendations to the SARFAESI valuation committee for a lower reserve price, and the property may be sold again by following the same procedures.

While discussing the procedure of the fixation of a reserve price, it is pertinent to examine how far the provisions are ensuring the fair price to the borrower and his views on the reserve price fixed by the authorised officer of the bank/FI. The valuation of the property by a registered valuer who is complying with the conditions stipulated in the rules is one of the measures in ensuring a fair price to the mortgagor. The committee system for the approval of reserve price is another measure to ensure fair price for the secured asset.

3. *Notice of sale*

A 30 day-notice of an intended sale is required to be given to the borrower/guarantor and in the case of the death of the borrower/guarantor, the sale notice should be addressed to the legal heirs of the borrowers/guarantors. The sale can be conducted only after expiry of the 30 day-notice given to borrower/guarantor and the legal heirs of borrowers/guarantors.

It is well within the discretion of the secured creditor/bank to proceed against the guarantors(s) or sell his assets without first taking any of the measures specified in Section 13(4) in relation to the secured assets (mortgage/hypothecation/charge) of the borrower under this Act.

4. *Sale procedure of movable property*

The authorised officer may sell the movable secured assets in one or more lots by any of the following methods to secure the maximum sale price for the assets:

- by obtaining a quotation from parties dealing with secured assets or otherwise interested in buying the secured assets
- by inviting tenders from the public
- by holding a public auction
- by private treaty.

The authorised officer shall serve to the borrower a notice of 30 days for the sale of the movable secured assets. If the sale of such secured assets is being effected either by inviting tenders or by holding a public auction, the secured creditor shall make a public notice in two leading newspapers, one in the vernacular language having sufficient circulation in the locality by setting out the terms of sale which shall include the following:

(1) Details about the borrower and the secured creditor;
(2) Description of movable secured assets to be sold with identification marks or numbers, if any, on them;
(3) Reserve price, if any, and the time and manner of payment;
(4) Time and place of the public auction or the time after which the sale by any other mode shall be completed;
(5) Depositing earnest money as may be stipulated by the secured creditor;
(6) Any other thing that the authorised officer considers material for a purchaser to know in order to judge the nature and value of movable secured assets.

It is important to note that the sale by any methods other than public auction or public tender shall be on such terms as may be settled between the parties in writing, i.e. between the secured creditor (bank) and the proposed purchaser in writing.

On payment of sale price, the authorised officer shall issue a certificate of sale in the prescribed form specifying the movable secured assets sold, price paid and the name of the purchaser, and thereafter sale shall become absolute. The certificate of sale so issued shall be prima facie evidence of the title of the purchaser.

5. *Sale procedures of immovable property*

The authorised officer shall take or cause to taken possession of by delivering a possession notice to the borrower and by affixing the possession notice on the outer door or at a conspicuous place on the property.

The authorised officer shall also publish the possession notice as soon as possible, but in any case not later than 7 days from the date of taking possession, in two leading newspapers, one in vernacular language having sufficient circulation in that locality.

In the event of actual possession of immovable property by the authorised officer, such property shall be kept in his own custody or in the custody of any person authorised or appointed by him, who shall take as much care of the property in his custody as an owner of ordinary prudence would, under the similar circumstances, take of such property. The authorised officer shall take steps for the preservation and protection of secured assets and insure them, if necessary, till they are sold or otherwise disposed of.

Before effecting a sale of the immovable property, the authorised officer shall obtain a valuation of the property from an approved valuer and in consultation with the secured creditor, fix the reserve price of the property and may sell the whole or any part of such immovable secured asset by any of the following methods:

- by obtaining quotations from the persons dealing with similar secured assets or otherwise interested in buying such assets
- by inviting tenders from the public
- by holding public auction
- by private treaty.

The authorised officer shall serve to the borrower a notice of 30 days for the sale of the immovable secured assets. If the sale of the secured asset is being effected by either inviting tenders from the public or by holding a public auction, the secured creditor shall place a public notice in two leading newspapers, one in vernacular language with sufficient circulation in the locality by setting out the terms of sale, which shall include

(1) The description of the immovable property to be sold, including details of the encumbrances known to the secured creditor;
(2) The secured debt for recovery of which the property is to be sold;
(3) Reserved price below which the property may not be sold;
(4) Time and place of public auction or the time after which sale by any other mode shall be completed;

(5) Depositing earnest money as may be stipulated by the authorised officer of the secured creditor;
(6) Any other thing which the authorised officer considers material for a purchaser to know in order to judge the nature and value of the property.

As per the instructions of Government of India's Ministry of Finance, an auction under the SARFAESI Act needs to be conducted only in e-auction mode only. Every notice of sale shall be affixed on a conspicuous part of the immovable property and may, if the authorised officer deems it fit, be placed on the website of the secured creditor on the Internet. The sale by any method other than public auction or public tender shall be on such terms as may be settled between the parties in writing, i.e. between the secured creditor (bank) and the proposed purchaser in writing.

When the dues of the secured creditor bank, together with all costs, charges and expenses incurred by him, are tendered by the borrower/guarantor at any time before the date of publication of notice for public auction or inviting quotations or tender from public or private treaty for transfer by way of lease, assignment or sale of the secured assets, the secured asset shall not be sold or transferred by the secured creditor bank, and no further steps shall be taken for the transfer or sale of that secured asset. The sale shall be confirmed only in favour of the highest bidder, and the sale confirmation letter must be issued to the successful bidder.

The sale cannot be confirmed if the sale price is less than the reserve price fixed.

The purchaser shall immediately, i.e. on the same day or not later than next working day, as the case may be, pay a deposit of 25% of the sale price, which is inclusive of earnest money deposited and balance to be paid on or before 15 days or any extended period agreed in writing between the purchaser and the bank in any case not exceeding three months. If the balance is not paid within the stipulated time, the deposit shall be forfeited, and steps should be taken to resell the property. The defaulting purchaser shall forfeit all claims to the property or to any part of the sum for which it may be subsequently sold. The authorised officer shall deliver the property to the purchaser free from encumbrances known to the secured creditor on deposit of the money as specified.

6. *Issue of a sale certificate*

If the sale proceeds are more than the reserve price, the sale may be confirmed by the authorised officer. On compliance with all the terms and conditions of sale and on deposit of the sale proceeds in full, the sale shall be confirmed in favour of the purchaser. A sale certificate is to be issued in favour of the purchaser, and in the sale certificate, it should mention specifically whether or not the purchaser has purchased the property free from encumbrances.

Where there are prior encumbrances, the purchaser should be asked to deposit such an amount to clear the encumbrances before issuing the sale certificate. If there is any surplus available out of the money deposited by the purchaser, such surplus shall be paid to the purchaser within 15 days from the date of finalisation of the sale. The sale of movable/immovable properties will be subject to payment of local taxes and a stamp duty on the documents prepared for effecting sale including the sale certificate as per the state/local laws.

7. *Recovery of shortfall, if any*

All the monies recovered shall be first applied in payment of costs, charges and expenses incurred in connection with proceedings initiated under this Act and, secondly, in the discharge of the dues of the bank; the remaining money so received shall be paid to the person entitled. The surplus money after the completion of the sale must be paid to the borrower/guarantor, who is the owner of the property.

If there is a shortfall in recovery of the debt due by the borrower, an application should be filed before the Debt Recovery Tribunal within whose jurisdiction the case falls.

8. *Jurisdiction of civil court barred*

Under Section 34 of the Act, the civil courts are barred from entertaining any suit or proceeding where Debt Recovery Tribunal is empowered to determine. The Hon'ble High Courts held in a number of cases that no injunction shall be granted by any civil court in respect of any action taken in pursuance of any power conferred under this Act.

9. *Application before the Debt Recovery Tribunal (DRT)*

Any person aggrieved by any measure taken by a secured creditor or his application authorised officer under Section 13(4) of the SARFAESI Act may file an appeal to the Debts Recovery Tribunal, within 45 days from the date on which such measure was taken. However, non-acceptance of representation or objection by the authorised officer/bank shall not entitle the borrower/guarantor to make an application to the Debt Recovery Tribunal. In terms of Section 17(5) of the SARFAESI Act, the DRT is required to dispose the application normally within 60 days, however, maximum within 4 months from the date of the application.

10. Debt Recovery Appellate Tribunal

If a person is aggrieved by the order of the DRT, he can file an appeal to the Appellate Tribunal within 30 days from date of receipt of the DRT order.

11. Exemptions from the Act

The provision of the Act shall not apply to the following:

(1) A lien on any goods, money or security given by or under the Indian Contract Act, 1872, or the Sale of Goods Act, or any other law for the time being in force;
(2) A pledge of movables within the meaning of Section 172 of Indian Contract Act;
(3) Creation of any security in any aircraft as defined u/s 2(1) of the Aircraft Act;
(4) Creation of any security interest in any vessel as defined in Section 3(35) of the Merchant Shipping Act;
(5) Any right of unpaid seller u/s 47 of the Sale of Goods Act;
(6) Any properties not liable to attachment or sale under first provision to Section 60(1) of the Code of Civil Procedure;
(7) Any security interest for securing repayment of any financial asset not exceeding 1 lakh rupee;
(8) Any security interest created in agricultural land;
(9) Any case in which the amount due is less than 20% of the principal amount and interest thereon (i.e. where borrower has repaid more than 80% of principal amount and interest).

12. Assistance of the chief metropolitan magistrate or district magistrate in taking possession of secured asset

The secured creditor can take possession of assets after 60 days from the receipt of the notice. Where possession of assets is required to be taken or if any asset is required to be sold or transferred and expects any resistance or law and order problems, the secured creditor may file the necessary applications before the chief metropolitan magistrate/chief judicial magistrate or the district magistrate within whose jurisdiction the assets are located to take possession of the assets. The chief metropolitan magistrate shall appoint an advocate commissioner on the application of the bank for taking possession of the property with the assistance of the police and will hand over to the bank. The bank is also entitled to approach the district magistrate who in turn can issue the necessary direction for taking possession with the assistance of the police.

13. *Change of directors/appointment of administrator*

With the management being taken over, the secured creditor can change the directors of the borrower company, if the borrower is a company, and appoint an administrator if the borrower is not a company. A notice to this effect should also be published in the newspaper. On publishing such a notice, the earlier directors (in case of a company) and persons holding any office of power of superintendence (if borrower is not a company) shall be deemed to have vacated their office. Any contract of management that the borrower had with any director or manager of the borrower's holding office shall be deemed to be terminated. The new directors/administrator appointed by the secured creditor will take custody or control all the property, effects or actionable claims to which the business of the borrower is entitled. The new directors/administrator shall alone be entitled to exercise all the powers of superintendence, direction and control of the business of the borrower.

14. *Effects of a takeover of management*

- Shareholders cannot appoint directors: After the takeover of assets, the shareholders of the company cannot appoint or nominate any director of the company.
- No resolution without the consent of the secured creditors: Any resolution passed by the shareholders will be effective only if approved by the secured creditors.
- No proceedings for winding up: No proceeding for winding up the company or an appointment of receiver shall lie in any court without the consent of secured creditor.
- No compensation for the loss of office: Any managing director or director of the borrower shall not be entitled to any compensation for loss of office or for premature termination of any contract or agreement with the borrower.

In the case of the financing of a financial asset by more than one secured creditors or joint financing of a financial asset by secured creditors, no secured creditor shall be entitled to excise any or all of the rights conferred on him under or pursuant to Sub-Section (4) unless the exercise of such rights are agreed upon by the secured creditors representing not less than 60% of the value of the amount outstanding as on a record date, and such action shall be binding on all the secured creditors.

15. *Protection of action taken in good faith*

Under Section 32 of the Act, no suit, prosecution or other legal proceedings shall lie against any secured creditor or any of his officers or managers exercising any of the rights of the secured creditor by the borrower/guarantor for anything done or omitted to be done in good faith under this act.

16. Limitation period

Under Section 36 of the Act, the secured creditor shall be entitled to take all or any of the measures under Sub-Section (4) of Section 13 of the Act unless his claim to the financial asset is made within the period of the limitation prescribed under the limitation act. Therefore, wherever any claim is barred by limitation, the claim under this law shall not be applicable. The secured creditors cannot exercise the rights under this act in respect to time barred debts.

IV. Lok Adalat

Lok Adalat is playing an important role in the settlement of disputes in the banking sector. The Legal Services Authorities Act, 1987, paved the way for administering justice without resorting to courts. It is a voluntary process and works on the principle that both parties to the dispute are willing to sort out their dispute amicably. Through this mechanism, disputes can be settled in a simple, quick and cost-effective way. Lok Adalats are conducted by state level, district level and taluk level legal services authorities in the respective states. The bank branches need to identify the accounts which can be referred to Lok Adalat.

The settlement of accounts in Lok Adalat will benefit the Banks in four ways:

- The award passed in Lok Adalat is at par with the decree by the civil court and is legally enforceable.
- Since no court fee and advocate fee is required for Lok Adalat, both the bank and the borrowers/guarantors can save court fees and advocate fees.
- It saves enormous time for the bank and the borrowers/guarantors as there is no need to go through the lengthy and time-consuming legal process.
- In suits filed cases, the Bank is entitled to receive a refund of the court fee by filing a suitable application through bank's advocate.

In view of the aforesaid advantages of Lok Adalat *vis-à-vis* the long drawn legal proceedings, both the bank and borrowers/guarantors can resort to Lok Adalat in bigger way to reduce the level of NPAs in banking sector.

V. Revenue Recovery Act

In some states, the Revenue Recovery Act has been made applicable to banks. In the State of Kerala, the provisions of the Kerala Revenue Recovery Act,

1968 have been made applicable to the priority sector lending up to the amount of Rs.20 lakhs. The Hon'ble High Court of Kerala has held in Bank of India v. Barry Sebastian[5] that the bank can resort to recovery proceedings under the Revenue Recovery Act in case of default. The Hon'ble High Court of Kerala has held in Jabbar and Another v. Dhanalakshmi Bank Ltd. and others[6] that advance granted to private retail traders of credit limits not exceeding Rs.5 lakhs would be considered to be a priority sector advance. Such sector advances could be recovered under the provisions of the Revenue Recovery Act. Since the Revenue Recovery Proceedings are also an expeditious process of adjudicating claims, Banks may make effective use of this platform for recovery of the bank's dues.

The NPAs in banks need to be promptly tackled through a double pronged approach viz. preventive and curative measures by banks at macro and micro levels. This may include a well-structured NPA management policy, the formulation of a risk rating system, the introduction of a pre-disbursement audit, credit audit system for large advances and systems to tackle potential problem loans. Further, maximising recovery through transparent compromise proposals, setting up internal committees at different levels in the Bank for quick disposals of settlement proposals and forming special recovery/NPA cells at controlling offices will accelerate the pace of recovery. Actions such as making concerned staff accountable for recovery and opening specialised rehabilitation branches for providing focussed attention to SARFAESI cases and cases marked for recovery through legal means may also, help in this regard. Upgrading information technology will facilitate better credit administration and help share vital information between branches as well as between banks and Financial Institutions and this should be the priority area for Bank managements. The bank should also start playing the role of a friend, philosopher and guide by counselling corporate borrowers to sell assets not necessary for their core areas of production/competence. It is of the utmost importance that necessary changes are brought about in the related legislations to make the recovery process smoother and less time consuming and to create other alternative channels/agencies for the recovery of debt/reduction of non-performing assets. As the Lok Adalat's have proved to be a good agency for quick justice and the recovery of smaller loans, their use could go a long way as a supplement to the efforts of recovery by the DRTs. To accelerate the recovery process, asset reconstruction companies can also play a vital role in the reduction of NPAs and thereby provide necessary liquidity to banks through the securitisation of the bank's loan assets.

Conclusion

In the course of recovery of dues through the legal process, there are two important legislations: the Recovery of Debts and Bankruptcy Act, 1993 (RDB Act) and the Securitisation and Reconstruction of Financial Assets and Enforcement of Security Interest Act (SARFAESI Act), 2002. The provisions of RDB Act have been framed to expedite the legal proceedings for adjudication of banks' dues above Rs.20 lakhs. For dues below Rs.20 lakhs, the civil courts with necessary jurisdiction will adjudicate such claims. Since the adjudication proceedings by the Debt Recovery Tribunals were not able to deliver results, the Union of India came up with the SARFAESI Act, which enabled the banks to take possession and conduct sales of property without approaching the courts or tribunals. The Lok Adalat's constituted under the Legal Services Authority Act and the Revenue Recovery Laws have also contributed to the recovery of debts dues to the banks.

****

Notes

1 Study group report from the website www.rbi.org.in.
2 Appeal (Civil) 3228 of 2006 – M/s. Transcore v. Union of India & Another.
3 Appeal (Civil) 3228 of 2006 – M/s. Transcore v. Union of India & Another.
4 Security Interest (Enforcement) (Amendment) Rules, 2007-S.O. 1837(E) dated 26 October 2007 – SARFAESI Act 2002.
5 Bank of India v. Barry Sebastian, 2013(1) KHC 584.
6 Jabbar and Another v. Dhanalakshmi Bank Ltd. and others, 2005 KHC 898.

Chapter 5

The role of judiciary in interpreting and establishing recovery laws relating to banking institutions

The banks and financial institutions operating in our country are required to comply with all the laws and rules laid down in various Indian statutes such as the Banking Regulations Act, the Reserve Bank of India Act, the Indian Contract Act, the Transfer of Property Act, the SARFAESI Act, the DRT Act, etc. Apart from the laws and rules laid down in the statutes, the banks and financial institutions are equally bound to follow the judgements of the Supreme Court and High Courts, which are also laws of the land. In terms of Article 141 of the Constitution of India, judgements delivered by the Supreme Court of India are laws and binding precedents on all banking and financial institutions operating in our country. Of late, the Supreme Courts and High Courts have passed judgements that are of high important and relevant to the area of operations today. The judgements of the Supreme Court in *Mardia Chemicals Ltd v. Union of India*[1] and in *Transcore v. Union of India and Another*[2] are a few instances of such landmark judgements on this point. In fact, the judgement in the Mardia Chemicals case upholds the constitutionality of the SARFEASI Act, whereby the banks/FIs were allowed to act independently without approaching the courts of law. Further, the judgement in the Transcore case empowered the banks/FIs to initiate simultaneous proceedings both under the SAREASI Act and the DRT Act.

In this chapter, the legal implications of various judgements of the Hon'ble Supreme Court and High Courts pertaining to the laws with respect to the recovery of dues to the banks and financial institutions with special reference to the SARFAESI Act and how such judgements helped in developing the present legal system will be discussed in detail.

I. *Mardia Chemicals Ltd v. Union of India*

In the landmark judgement delivered in *Mardia Chemicals Ltd v. Union of India*, the Hon'ble Supreme Court of India held that the provisions of the Securitisation and Reconstruction of Financial Assets and Enforcement of Security

DOI: 10.4324/9781003546238-5

Interest Act, 2002 (the SARFEASI Act) are valid except Sub-Section (2) of Section 17, which is *ultra vires* of Article 14 of the Constitution of India.

1. *The main contention of the petitioner borrower*

The petitioner challenged the constitutional validity of the SARFEASI Act. The main contention challenging the vires of the provisions of the Act was that the banks and the financial institutions have been vested with arbitrary powers without guidelines for their exercise and also without providing any appropriate and adequate mechanism to decide the disputes relating to the correctness of the demand, its validity and the actual amount of the dues sought to be recovered from the borrowers. The further contentions put forwarded by the petitioner are as follows:

- The SARFEASI Act has been made a one-sided affair while enforcing drastic measures of the sale of property or taking over the management of the possession of the secured assets without affording any opportunity to the borrower.
- There was no occasion to enact such a draconian legislation to find a short-cut to realise the dues, without the borrower's ascertainment but only on the basis on which the secured creditor considered the dues and declare the same as NPAs.
- There is already a special enactment providing for the recovery of dues for banks and financial institutions, i.e. the DRT Act.
- No provision has been made to take into account the lender's liability, although at one time it was considered necessary to have an enactment relating to lender's liability, and a bill was also intended to be introduced, as it was considered necessary for the lenders to conduct themselves responsibly towards the borrowers. No such law has been enacted so far, nor has any care been taken to introduce such safeguards in the SARFEASI Act to protect the borrowers against their vulnerability to arbitrary or irresponsible action on the part of the lenders. The mechanism provided for the recovery of the debt under Section 13 does not provide for any adjudicatory forum to resolve any dispute which may arise in relation to the liability of the borrower to be treated as a defaulter or to see if there has been any violation or lapse on the part of the creditor or in regard to the correctness of the amount sought to be recovered and the interest levied thereupon.
- The provision of an appeal contained in Section 17 of the SARFEASI Act is illusory since the appeal would be maintainable after the possession of the property or the management of the secured assets has been taken over or the property has been sold. Further, an appeal is not entertainable unless 75% of the amount claimed in the notice is deposited by the borrower with the Debt Recovery Tribunal.

2. *The main contention of the respondent bank*

The respondents, primarily the banks, put forward the following line of arguments in favour of enactment of the SARFEASI Act:

- The SAREASI Act was enacted to curb the menace of growing NPAs. It affects the banks and financial institutions, which is ultimately against the public interest. Since the recovery through DRT was not encouraging, a need was felt for a faster procedure empowering the secured creditors to recover their dues and for the securitisation of financial assets so as to generate maximum monetary liquidity.
- If the borrower wants to raise any objection against Section 13(2) of the SARFEASI Act, it may be raised in reply to the notice, which would obviously be considered by the secured creditor before it would further proceed to take recourse to Sub-Section 4 of Section 13 of the Act. So an opportunity has been provided to the borrower under the provisions of the Act.
- The proviso to Section 17 very clearly provides that on an application, the condition of deposit of amount can be waived or the amount can be reduced. Therefore, it would not be correct to say that the condition of a pre-deposit is harsh as it can relaxed in deserving cases.
- The bar of jurisdiction of the civil court was thought to be necessary to avoid a lengthy legal process in realising the amount due.

3. *The main questions for consideration by the court*

Taking the overall view of the rival contentions of the parties in the case, the Hon'ble Court drew the following main questions for consideration:

(1) Is it open to challenge the statute on the ground that it was not necessary to enact it in the prevailing background, particularly when another statute was already in operation?
(2) Did provisions as contained under Sections 13 and 17 of the Act provide adequate and efficacious mechanisms to consider and decide the objections/disputes raised by a borrower against the recovery, particularly in view of the bar to approach the civil court under Section 34 of the Act?
(3) Is the remedy available under Section 17 of the Act illusory for the reason that it is available only after the action is taken under Section 13(4) of the Act and the appeal would be entertainable only on a deposit of 75% of the claim raised in the notice of demand?
(4) Could the terms or existing rights under the contract entered into by two private parties be amended by the provisions of law providing certain powers in one-sided manner in favour of one of the parties to the contract?

(5) Are the provision for the sale of the properties without the intervention of the court under Section 13 of the Act akin to the English mortgage and its effect on the scope of the bar of the jurisdiction of the civil court?
(6) Are the provisions under Sections 13 and 17(2) of the Act unconstitutional on the basis of the parameters laid down in different decisions of this court?
(7) Has the principle of lender's liability been absolutely ignored while enacting the Act and its effect?

4. *The ratio of judgement of the court*

In regard to the first question, the Hon'ble Court held that in the present day of the global economy, it may be difficult to stick to old and conventional methods of financing and recovery of dues. Hence, it cannot be said that a step taken towards securitisation of the debts and to evolve means for the faster recovery of the NPAs was not called for or that it was a superimposition of the undesired law since one legislation was already operating in the field, namely the Recovery of Debts Due to Banks and Financial Institutions Act. Considering the totality of circumstances in the financial climate worldwide, if it was thought of as a matter of policy to have a speedier legal method to recover the dues, such a policy decision cannot be faulted nor is it a matter to be sent to the courts to test the legitimacy of such a measure relating to financial policy.

With respect to the second question, the Hon'ble Court held that a policy has been laid down by the Reserve Bank of India providing guidelines in the matter of declaring an asset to be a non-performing asset, which is known as the "RBI's Prudential Norms on Income Recognition, Asset Classification and Provisioning Pertaining to Advances". In terms of the RBI's circular, an asset, including a leased asset, becomes non-performing when it ceases to generate income for the bank. Since the terms and conditions and circumstances in which the debt is to be classified as a non-performing asset was laid down by the Reserve Bank of India, the Hon'ble Court found no substance in the submission of the petitioners that there were no guidelines for treating the debt as a non-performing asset.

While dealing with the third question, the Hon'ble Court held that the amount of deposit of 75% of the demand, at the initial proceedings itself, was unreasonable and oppressive. The requirement of a deposit of such a heavy amount on the basis of a one-sided claim alone cannot be said to be a reasonable condition at the first instance itself before start of the adjudication of the dispute. Merely giving power to the Tribunal to waive or reduce the amount did not cure the inherent infirmity leaning one-sidedly in favour of the party who, so far, has alone been the party to decide the amount and the fact of default and to classify the dues a NPAs without the participation/association of the borrower in the process.

In regards to the fourth question, the Hon'ble Court held that although the transaction may have a character of a private contract, the question of great importance behind such transactions as a whole has a far reaching effect on the economy of the country and cannot be ignored by purely restricting it to individual transactions, more particularly when financing is through banks and financial institutions utilising the money of the people in general, namely, the depositors in the banks and public money at the disposal of the financial institutions. Therefore, wherever public interest to such a large extent is involved and it may become necessary to achieve an objective which serves public purposes, individual rights may have to give way. Public interest has always been considered to be above private interest.

While dealing with the fifth question, the Hon'ble Court held that Section 13 of the SARFEASI Act overrides the provisions contained in Section 69 of the Transfer of Property Act, where it is said that in no cases, other than those as enumerated in Clauses (a), (b) and (c) of Section 69, a mortgage shall be enforced without the intervention of the court. Once the condition given in Section 69 of the TP Act, the general law on the subject was overridden by the special enactment, namely, the Securitization Act, and it would not make much of a difference as to whether or not the transactions in question are akin to or amount to an English mortgage because irrespective of the kind of the mortgage, the secured interest is liable to be enforced without intervention of the court as per the provision contained under Section 13 of the Act.

While addressing the sixth and seventh questions, the Hon'ble Court held that on measures having been taken under Sub-Section (4) of Section 13 and before the date of sale/auction of the property, it would be open for the borrower to file an appeal under Section 17 of the SAREASI Act before the Debt Recovery Tribunal. After service of the 13(2) notice, if the borrower raises any objection or places facts for the consideration of the secured creditor, such a reply to the notice must be considered with due application of mind, and the reasons for not accepting the objections, however brief they may be, must be communicated to the borrower. The Hon'ble Court held that the effects of some of the provisions may be a bit harsh for some of the borrowers, but on that ground the impugned provisions of the SARFEASI Act cannot be said to be unconstitutional in view of the fact that the objective of the Act is to achieve a speedier recovery of the dues declared as NPAs and better availability of capital liquidity and resources to help in the growth of economy of the country and the welfare of the people in general, which would subserve the public interest. In this connection, the Hon'ble Court also referred to the observations made in *Collector of Customs, Madras v. Nathella Samapathu*[3] wherein it was held that the intent of the Parliament shall not be defeated merely for the reason that it may operate a bit harshly on a small section of public. In another decision, i.e. *Kishanchand Arora v. Commissioner of*

Police,[4] it was held that the absence of an appeal does not necessarily render the legislation unreasonable. However, the Hon'ble Court held that the requirement of deposit of 75% of the amount before entertaining an appeal under Section 17 of the Act was an oppressive, onerous and arbitrary condition against all the cannons of reasonableness. Such a condition is invalid, and it is liable to be struck down. Accordingly, the Hon'ble Court upheld the validity of the SARFEASI Act and its provisions except that of Sub-Section (2) of Section 17 of the Act, which was declared *ultra vires* of Article 14 of the Constitution of India.

II. *Transcore v. Union of India and Another*

The Hon'ble Supreme Court of India in its landmark judgement in *Transcore v. Union of India and Another*[5] held that withdrawal of a suit pending before DRT is not a pre-condition for taking recourse to the SARFEASI Act. This judgement is prominent in the sense that it cleared the legal conundrum regarding the initiation of simultaneous proceedings under the DRT Act and the SARFAESI Act. This judgement permitted the banks/FIs to proceed under the SARFEASI Act simultaneously without withdrawing the OA filed before the DRT. The moot question, whether the withdrawal of OA in terms of the first proviso to Section 19(1) of the DRT Act, 1993, is a condition precedent to take recourse to the SARFEASI Act and Rules, 2002, came for consideration before JJ. Arijit Pasayat and S.H. Kapadia of the Hon'ble Supreme Court of India. The Hon'ble Supreme Court held that the withdrawal of a suit pending before the DRT is not a pre-condition for taking recourse to the SARFEASI Act. The remedy under the SARFEASI Act is an additional remedy, which is not inconsistent with the DRT Act, 1993, and, therefore, the doctrine of election has no application.

1. *The main contention of the petitioner borrower*

In this case, the Indian Overseas Bank, respondent herein, issued a possession notice under Section 13(4) of the SARFEASI Act upon the appellant company calling for repayment of the default amount. The appellant company contended that the respondent bank could not have invoked the SARFEASI Act without the prior permission of the DRT before whom OA was pending. The appellant company further contended that the respondent bank is duty bound and obliged to make an application to the DRT seeking a withdrawal of OA. The first proviso to Section 19(1) of the DRT Act states that the bank or financial institution may, with the permission of the DRT, by application, withdraw the OA made before or after the amending Act 30 of 2004 for the purpose of taking action under the SARFEASI Act, 2002, if no such action had been taken earlier under that Act.

2. *The main contention of the respondent bank*

The respondent bank argued that the said proviso is an enabling provision; banks and financial institutions have an independent right to recover debts. The purpose behind enactment of the NPA Act was to obliterate all fetters on their right to recover the debt which earlier existed in the form of Sections 69 and 69A of the Transfer of Property Act, 1882, and consequently, the option lay with the banks/FIs to invoke or not to invoke the SARFEASI Act. The respondent bank further argued that they were not mandatorily obliged to obtain the prior leave of the DRT and that the said proviso is not a condition precedent to taking recourse to the NPA Act.

3. *The main questions for consideration by the court*

In this case, the Hon'ble Supreme Court settled on the following points for determination:

(1) Can the banks or financial institutions, having elected to seek their remedy in terms of DRT Act, 1993, still invoke the SARFEASI Act, 2002, to realise the secured assets without withdrawing or abandoning the OA filed before the DRT under the DRT Act?
(2) Does recourse to take possession of the secured assets of the borrower in terms of Section 13(4) of the SARFEASI Act comprehend the power to take actual possession of the immovable property?
(3) Is the ad valorem court fee prescribed under Rule 7 of the DRT (Procedure) Rules, 1993, payable on an application under Section 17(1) of the SARFEASI Act in the absence of any rule framed under the said Act?

At first, the Hon'ble Supreme Court examined the doctrine of election. The Hon'ble Court held that there are three elements of election, namely, the existence of two or more remedies; inconsistencies between such remedies; and a choice of one of them. If any one of the three elements is not there, the doctrine will not apply. In the present case, the SARFEASI Act is an additional remedy to the DRT Act. Together they constitute one remedy, and therefore, the doctrine of election does not apply.

The Hon'ble Court further held that the SARFEASI Act was enacted to enforce the interest in the financial assets which belongs to the bank/FI by virtue of the contract between the parties or by operation of common law principles or by law. The very objective of Section 13 of the SARFEASI Act is recovery by non-adjudicatory process. A secured asset under the SARFEASI Act is an asset in which interest is created by the borrower in favour of the bank/FI, and on that basis alone the SARFEASI Act seeks to enforce the security interest by a non-adjudicatory process. The SARFEASI Act proceeds on the basis that the debtor has failed not only to repay the debt, but he has also failed to maintain the level of margin and to maintain value of the security at that level. It is for this reason that Sections 13(1) and 13(2) of the SARFEASI Act proceed on the basis that the security interest in the banks/FIs needs to be enforced expeditiously without the intervention of the court/tribunal; the liability of the borrower has accrued and on account of the default in repayment, the account of the borrower in the books of the bank has become non-performing. Therefore, the SARFEASI Act states that the enforcement could take place by non-adjudicatory process and the Act removes all fetters under the aforementioned circumstances on the rights of the secured creditor.

The Hon'ble Court held that withdrawal of the OA pending before the DRT under the DRT Act is not a pre-condition for taking recourse to the SARFEASI Act. It is for the bank/FI to exercise its discretion as to cases in which it may apply for leave and in cases where they may not apply for leave to withdraw.

With respect to the second question for determination, i.e. whether recourse to take possession of the secured assets of the borrower in terms of Section 13(4) of the SARFEASI Act comprehends the power to take actual possession of the immovable property, the Hon'ble Court held that the authorised officer under Rule 8 has greater powers than even a court receiver as security interest in the property already created in favour of the banks/FI. Rule 8 provides that till issuance of the sale certificate under Rule 9, the authorised officer shall take such steps as he deems fit to preserve the secured asset.

In view of the aforesaid grounds, the Hon'ble Court dismissed the appeal filed by the borrower, M/s. Transcore, and the appeal filed by the banks/FIs stands allowed.

III. *Authorised Officer, Indian Overseas Bank and Another v. Ashok Saw Mill*

The main question which falls for determination before the Hon'ble Supreme Court in *Authorised Officer, Indian Overseas Bank and Another v. Ashok Saw Mill*[6] is whether the DRT would have jurisdiction to consider and adjudicate with regard to post 13(4) events or whether its scope in terms of Section 17 of the SARFEASI Act would be confined to the stage contemplated under Section 13(4), as contended on behalf of the appellants.

The respondent firm and its sister concern, Ashok Woodworks, availed various loans from the appellant bank which were secured by movable and immovable assets. The loanee firms defaulted in repayment of the loans, and since their accounts became NPAs, the bank initiated action against them under the provisions of the SAREASI Act and issued separate demand notices to the respondent partnership firm and its sister concern under Section 13(2) of SARFEASI Act. As the respondent and its sister concern did not respond to the demand notices, the appellant bank invoked Section 13(4) of the SAR-EASI Act and took possession of the secured assets. The said action of the appellant bank, as also the vires of the SARFEASI Act, were challenged by the respondent firm and its sister concern by way of two separate writ petitions. The said writ petitions were ultimately heard and dismissed with liberty to the respondent firm to approach the Debts Recovery Tribunal. Because, despite a liberty, the respondent firm did not approach the DRT, the bank made a decision to sell the secured assets of the respondent firm. The same was challenged by the respondent firm in a writ petition. After hearing the parties, the High Court refused to grant any interim relief and posted the writ petition for final disposal.

During the pendency of the said writ petition, the respondent firm, along with Ashok Woodworks, filed a SARFEASI application before the DRT at Madurai on the self-same cause of action. Despite being informed of the pendency of the writ petition for the self-same reliefs, the Tribunal, by its order, directed the bank to defer the proposed sale. The appellant bank thereupon filed a civil writ petition before the High Court challenging the filing of the SARFEASI application. The same was admitted, and all proceedings in the SAREASI application were stayed. The appellant bank was permitted to open the sealed tenders which it had received pursuant to the sale notice, subject to the condition that the sale effected would be subject to the confirmation of the court. Aggrieved by the said order, the bank filed a writ appeal, which was dismissed by the division bench against which the present appeal presented before the Hon'ble Supreme Court.

The Hon'ble Supreme Court held that intention of the Legislature is clear that while the banks/FIs have been vested with stringent powers for the recovery of their dues, safeguards have also been provided to rectify any error or wrongful use of such powers by vesting the DRT with the authority after conducting an adjudication into the matter to declare any such action invalid and also to restore possession even though the possession may have been made over to the transferee. The consequences of the authority vested in the DRT under Sub-Section (3) of Section 17 necessarily implies that the DRT is entitled to question the action taken by the secured creditor and the transactions entered into by virtue of Section 13(A) of the Act. The Legislature, by including Sub-Section (3) in Section 17, went to the extent of vesting the DRT with authority to even set aside a transaction including a sale and to restore possession to the borrower in appropriate cases. Resultantly, the submissions advanced by the appellant bank that the DRT has no jurisdiction to deal with a post-13(4) situation cannot be accepted. The law contemplated that the action taken by a secured creditor in terms of Section 13(4) is open to scrutiny and cannot only be set aside but even the *status quo ante* can be restored by the DRT. With these findings, the Hon'ble Court saw no reason to interfere with the judgement, and the order of the High Court and the appeal was accordingly dismissed.

IV. *United Bank of India v. Satyawati Tondon and Others*

The Hon'ble Supreme Court of India, in its judgement on 26 July 2010 in *United Bank of India v. Satyawati Tondon and Others*,[7] held that despite the repeated pronouncement of the Supreme Court, the High Courts continue to ignore the availability of statutory remedies under the DRT Act and the SARFAESI Act and exercise jurisdiction under Article 226 for passing orders, which have serious adverse impact on the rights of banks and other financial institutions to recover their dues.

In the case on hand, the appellant bank sanctioned a term loan in favour of M/s. Pawan Color Lab and respondent no.1 gave a guarantee for repayment of the loan and mortgaged her property by the deposit of title deeds. The appellant bank issued a notice to respondents under Section 13(2) of the SARFAESI Act. Upon receipt of the notice, respondent no.1 offered to pay a sum of Rs.18 lakhs for settlement of the loan account, but the appellant bank did not accept the offer and filed an application under Section 14 of the SARFAESI Act, which was allowed by the district magistrate/collector. Thereafter, the appellant bank issued a notice to the respondent under Section 13(4) of the SARFEASI Act.

Faced with the imminent threat of losing the mortgaged property, respondent no.1 filed a Civil Mis. Writ petition asking for an order to restrain the appellant bank from taking coercive action in pursuance of the notices issued under Section 13(2) and (4) and the order passed by district magistrate/collector. The Division Bench of the High Court did not accept the appellant's plea that the writ petition should not be entertained because an alternative remedy was available to the writ petitioner under Section 17 of the SARFAESI Act, and it passed an order restraining the appellant from taking action in furtherance of the notice issued under Section 13(4) of the SARFAESI Act on the grounds that the bank should have proceeded against the borrower and exhausted all the remedies before proceeding against the guarantor.

While dealing with this special leave petition preferred by the appellant bank, the Hon'ble Supreme Court of India observed that the question of whether the appellant bank could have issued notices to the guarantor and filed an application under Section 14 of the SARFAESI Act without first initiating action against the borrower for recovery of the outstanding dues is no longer res integra.

The Hon'ble Supreme Court held that the High Court completely misdirected itself in assuming that the appellant could not have initiated action against the guarantor without making efforts for recovery of its dues from the borrower. Further, if the guarantor had any tangible grievance against the notice issued under Section 13(4) or action taken under Section 14, then the guarantor could have availed remedy by filing an application under Section 17(1) of SARFAESI Act. It is thus evident that the remedies available to an aggrieved person under the SARFAESI Act are both expeditious and effective. Unfortunately, the High Court overlooked the settled law that it will ordinarily not entertain a petition under Article 226 of the Constitution if an effective remedy is available to the aggrieved person and that this rule applies with greater rigour in matters involving the recovery of taxes, cess, fees, other types of public money and the dues of banks and other financial institutions. While dealing with the petitions involving challenge to the action taken for recovery of public dues, etc., the High Court must keep in mind that the legislations enacted by Parliament and state legislatures for recovery of such dues are code unto themselves in as much as they not only contain comprehensive procedure for the recovery of the dues but also envisage the constitution of quasi-judicial bodies for redressal of the grievance of any aggrieved person. Therefore, in all such cases, the High Court must insist that before availing remedy under Article 226 of the Constitution, a person must exhaust the remedies available under the relevant statute.

The Hon'ble Court held that in cases relating to recovery of the dues of banks, financial institutions and secured creditors, stay granted by the High Court would have serious adverse impact on the financial health of such bodies/institutions, which ultimately prove detrimental to the economy of the nation. Therefore, the High Court should be extremely careful and circumspect in exercising its discretion to grant stay in such matters. In *City and Industrial Development Corporation v. Dosu Aardeshir Bhiwandiwala and Others*[8] (2009) 1 SCC 168, the Hon'ble Supreme Court highlighted the parameters which are required to be kept in view by the High Court while exercising jurisdiction under Article 226 of the Constitution. The High Court, while exercising its jurisdiction under Article 226, is duty-bound to consider the following:

- Does the adjudication of writ petition involve any complex and disputed questions of facts and can they be satisfactorily resolved?
- Does the petition reveal all material facts?
- Does the petitioner have any alternative or effective remedy for the resolution of the dispute?
- Is the person invoking the jurisdiction guilty of unexplained delays and laches?
- Is it *ex facie* barred by any laws of limitation?
- Is the grant of relief against public policy or barred by any valid law or a host of other factors?

After analysing the aforesaid parameters and the factual matrix of the case, the Hon'ble Supreme Court held that the High Court was not at all justified in injuncting the appellant from taking action in furtherance of the notice issued under Section 13(4) of the Act. The Hon'ble Court further held that it is a matter of serious concern that despite repeated pronouncement of the Supreme Court, the High Courts continue to ignore the availability of statutory remedies under the DRT Act and the SARFAESI Act and exercise jurisdiction under Article 226 for passing orders which have a serious adverse impact on the rights of banks and other financial institutions to recover their dues. While disposing the special leave petition, the Hon'ble Supreme Court declared that it hopes and trusts that in future the High Courts will exercise their discretion in such matters with greater caution, care and circumspection.

V. *Eureka Forbes Limited v. Allahabad Bank and Others*

The question of whether the DRT has jurisdiction to entertain and decide the claim of the bank against a person who is neither a borrower nor has any kind of privity of contract between the bank and that person? It was discussed and decided by the Hon'ble Supreme Court of India in its judgement delivered on 3rd May 2010 in *Eureka Forbes Limited v. Allahabad Bank and Others*.[9] Ahead of discussing the legal nuances involved in this case, it would be appropriate to review the factual matrix of the case. A brief description of the factual matrix of the case is as follows:

The appellant company, M/s. Eureka Forbes Ltd, entered into an agreement with respondents, granting a licence in their favour to use the premises along with the plant and machinery as well as their trademark. The respondents had availed a certain cash credit facility and had hypothecated their raw materials and semi-finished products to Allahabad Bank. Since the respondents failed to pay the licence fee for the use and occupation of the premises, goods, etc., they requested the appellant company to take over the possession of the premises along with the closing stock lying therein. Meanwhile, the respondent bank wrote to the respondent and raised an issue as to how the possession of the stocks and machinery was given to the appellant company since they had a charge over the movable assets.

The bank filed suit against the appellant company and respondents for the recovery of bank's dues. Later, the case was transferred to the DRT. In the appeal filed by the appellant company, the Debt Recovery Appellate Tribunal directed the respondent bank to refund the sum appropriated from the appellant company together with interest at the lending rate.

The respondent bank challenged the order of the DRAT under Article 227 of the Constitution before the single judge of the Kolkata High Court, but the order of DRAT was restored by the single judge of the High Court. Aggrieved, the bank brought the appeal before the division bench of the Kolkata High Court, which by its order dismissed the appeal and sustained the order of the single judge. Again, aggrieved by the said order, the bank submitted a special leave petition before the Hon'ble Supreme Court.

After careful consideration of the factual matrix and legal issues involved in this case, the Hon'ble Supreme Court held that there was no dispute of the fact that goods had been hypothecated to the bank, and in spite of the complete knowledge of this fact, the appellant company went on to sell the goods. The bank had been negligent and, to some extent, irresponsible in invoking its rights and taking appropriate remedy in accordance with law.

The Hon'ble Court declared that mere irresponsibility, on the part of the bank, would not wipe out the rights of the bank in the law. Without the consent of the bank, no person can utilise the hypothecated goods for his own benefit or sale by the borrower or any person connected thereto. It is nobody's case that the bank had consented to such sale. Physical domain over the hypothecated goods is no way a sine qua non for enforcing the bank's rights against the borrower. It was obligatory upon the appellant to deal with the goods only with the leave and permission of the bank. Absence such consent in writing, it would obviously result in a breach of the bank's rights.

The Supreme Court further observed that in the event when a party which had pledged or mortgaged properties in favour of the bank transferred such properties in favour of a third party, the bank is entitled to takes action under the provisions of the DRT Act. Otherwise, it would be tantamount to a travesty of justice and would frustrate the very legislative objective and intent behind the provisions of the DRT Act. The Hon'ble Court held that the claim of the bank relatable to the hypothecated goods was well within the jurisdiction of the Tribunal exercising its power under Section 17 of the DRT Act.

VI. *Indian Bank v. Blue Jaggers Estates Ltd and Others*

The Hon'nble Supreme Court of India in its judgement delivered in *Indian Bank v. Blue Jaggers Estates Ltd and Others*[10] on 9th August 2010 held that the doctrine of an unconscionable contract cannot be invoked for frustrating the action initiated by the appellant bank for recovery of its dues.

The Supreme Court held that defaulting borrowers are using court process for frustrating the action initiated by the bank under the provisions of Securitisation and Reconstruction of Financial Assets and Enforcement of Security Interest Act, 2002, for recovery of its dues. The Hon'ble Supreme Court of India held that the appeals filed by the default borrowers in this case are illustrative of how a defaulting borrower can use the court process for frustrating the action initiated by the bank for recovery of its dues.

The appellant-bank sanctioned loan to N.S. Investments, a partnership firm and the account of N.S. Investments, was declared as a non-performing asset, and the respondent no.1, Blue Jaggers Estate Ltd, took over the assets and liabilities of N.S. Investments. Since the respondents failed to clear the outstanding dues, the appellant filed an application under Section 19 of the Recovery of Debts Due to Banks and Financial Institutions Act, 1993. Meanwhile, the appellant bank issued a notice under Section 13(2) of the SARFEASI Act. The respondents filed objections under Section 13(3-A) of the SARFEASI Act and claimed that during the pendency of the recovery proceedings instituted under the DRT Act, the appellant cannot invoke the provisions of the Act. The respondents filed application under Section 17 of the SARFEASI Act. The Ld. DRT dismissed the Section 17 application filed by the respondents. The respondents challenged the order of the Ld. DRT by filing an appeal under Section 18 of the SARFEASI Act. The Debts Recovery Appellate Tribunal granted an interim stay subject to the condition of deposit of Rs.3 crores in two equal instalments. Since the respondents did not comply with the order passed by the Appellate Tribunal, the authorised officer of the appellant bank auctioned some of the mortgaged properties. Thereafter, the respondents filed two writ petitions, one for quashing the order of the Appellate Tribunal and another for issue of a mandamus to the Tribunal to dispose of the original application. While disposing of the writ petitions, the Hon'ble Division Bench of the High Court not only set aside the interim order passed by the Appellate Tribunal, but it also declared that as a result of sale of the property worth Rs.5 crores, the requirement of a deposit of Rs.3 crores stood satisfied.

Aggrieved by the order of division bench of the Hon'ble High Court, the appellant bank approached the Hon'ble Supreme Court of India and argued that the division bench of the High Court did not have the jurisdiction to nullify the conditional interim order passed by the Appellate Tribunal as the writ petition filed against that order was dismissed by the High Court and the special leave petition was dismissed by the Supreme Court. Further, the High Court committed a serious error by taking note of the bids given at the auction for the purpose of relieving the respondents of their statutory obligation to deposit 50% of the debts due.

The Hon'ble Supreme Court held that the respondents cannot be allowed to indirectly question the correctness of the order of the Appellate Tribunal to deposit Rs.3 crores because the respondent's challenge to that order was negatived by the High Court and the Supreme Court. Another argument of the respondent was that the rate of interest is unconscionable, expropriatory and contrary to law and merits rejection because at no stage had the respondents questioned the terms on which loan and other financial facilities were extended by the appellant. The fact of the matter is that the respondents had signed the agreement with open eyes and agreed to abide by the terms on which the loan, etc. was offered by the appellant. Therefore, the doctrine of unconscionable contract cannot be invoked for frustrating the action initiated by the appellant for the recovery of its dues. Accordingly, the civil appeal filed by the appellant bank was allowed by the Hon'ble Supreme Court, and the impugned order of the High Court was set aside insofar as it declares that the direction given by the Appellate Tribunal to the respondents to deposit Rs.3 crores stands complied.

VII. *ICICI Bank v. Shanti Devi Sharma and Others*

The judgement of the Hon'ble Supreme Court in this case is an eye opener to the bank/financial institutions who are not complying with the rules and regulations for the recovery of dues from the borrowers. While dealing with the aforesaid criminal appeal arising out of SLP (Crl) no.4935 of 2006, decided on 15th May 2008, between ICICI Bank v. Shanti Devi Sharma and Others,[11] the Hon'ble Supreme Court of India reminded financial institutions that they are bound by law. The recovery of loans or seizure of vehicles can only be done through legal means. The Hon'ble Court further stated that we live in a civilised country and are governed by the rule of law.

The respondent in this criminal appeal had filed a criminal writ petition in the Delhi High Court seeking a writ of mandamus to direct the commissioner of police to take action against the ICICI Bank. The respondent alleged that her son committed suicide as a result of the manner in which the bank's recovery agents had repossessed her son's motorcycle. In the first information report, the respondent alleged that the recovery agents repossessed the vehicle in the presence of his friends who ridiculed him for having lost the motorcycle. The deceased son of the respondent finally broke down before his wife and allegedly stated that he had never faced such a humiliation/disgrace in his entire life and ultimately hung himself to death.

To ascertain the veracity of these assertions in the first information report, the Hon'ble High Court ordered the police to file reports as to the status of the investigation against the bank. The Hon'ble High Court reviewed the status reports and directed the investigating officer to conclude the investigation into the matter as expeditiously as possible and take necessary action against those who may be found guilty of abetting the deceased to commit suicide.

The Hon'ble Supreme Court also took this opportunity to remind the financial institutions that they are bound by law. The court further observed that the SARFAESI Act and the Security Interest (Enforcement) Rules, 2002 (SIER) provide some of the procedures by which security interests may be recovered. In addition to the SARFAESI and SIER, the Reserve Bank of India (RBI) has promulgated guidelines on the subject. The "RBI Guidelines on Fair Practices Code for Lenders" dated 5th May 2003 provides that in the matter of recovery of loans, the lenders should not resort to undue harassment viz. persistently bothering the borrowers at odd hours, use muscle power for recovery of loans, etc.

The RBI has also expressed its concern about the number of litigations filed against the banks in the recent past for engaging recovery agents who have purportedly violated the law. The RBI has stated that "banks, as principals, are responsible for the actions of their agents". Hence, they should ensure that their agents engaged for recovery of their dues should strictly adhere to the guidelines and instructions, including the "Code of Bank's Commitment to Customers" (BCSBI Code) pertaining to collection of dues, while engaged in the process of the recovery of dues.

Looking into the gravity of the allegations raised in the case, the Hon'ble Supreme Court directed an expedited investigation and further directed the appellant to pay the costs of the litigation to the respondents, which was quantified as Rs.25,000.

VIII. *Lakshmi Shankar Mills (P) Ltd. & Others v. Authorised Officer/Chief Manager, Indian Bank & Others*

The full bench of the Hon'ble Madras High Court in M/s *Lakshmi Shankar Mills (P) Ltd. & Others v. Authorised Officer/Chief Manager, Indian Bank & Others*[12] considered the following questions for determination:

(1) Even where no stay is requested by the borrower during pending of the proceedings under Section 17 before the Debt Recovery Tribunal, can the secured creditor proceed to auction the secured asset before a declaration envisaged under Section 17(4) of the SARFAESI Act?
(2) When granting any stay of auction, can the Debt Recovery Tribunals impose any condition relating to deposit?
(3) Even before the finalisation of the proceedings under Section 17 of the SARFAESI Act, does the Debt Recovery Tribunal or the Debt Recovery Appellate Tribunal have any incidental or ancillary power to pass any interim order relating to the restoration of possessions or restoration of management, subject to imposition of any reasonable condition as deemed fit and proper?
(4) What is the scope of enquiry under Section 17 of the SARFAESI Act, and can the merits of the contentions raised by the borrower be decided while dealings with the question relating to validity of the action taken by the bank under Section 13 of the Act.

While dealing with the first question, the Hon'ble Court held that there will be no automatic stays on filing of an application under Section 17 of the SARFAESI Act. The statement of objectives and reasons of the SARFAESI Act make it manifestly clear that the intention of the Act to discourage the borrowers to postpone the repayment of their dues and also to enable the secured creditor to speedily recover their dues, if required by enforcement of security or other measures specified in Sub-Section (4) of Section 13 of the Act. It is well known that when the Legislature wants to grant a statutory stay, it would expressly say so. There is nothing in Section 17 of the SARFAESI Act that would indicate that the Legislature intended that there would be automatic stay of proceedings under Section 13(4) on filing an application under Section 17.

In regard to the second question, the Hon'ble Court held that there is no specific provision made under Section 17 of the SARFAESI Act or under any other provisions of the said Act empowering the Tribunal to pass any interim order. But under Sub-Section (12) of Section 19 of the Recovery of Debts Due to Banks and Financial Institutions Act, 1993, the Tribunal has been empowered to pass various interim orders. If Sub-Section (7) of Section 17 of the SARFAESI Act is read along with Sub-Section (12) of Section 19 of the Recovery of Debts Due to Banks and Financial Institutions Act, it would be clear that the Tribunal also has jurisdiction to pass interim orders under Section 17 of the SARFAESI Act in appropriate cases. The Hon'ble Court further held that while granting stay of auction, the Tribunal can impose a condition relating to deposit.

While dealing with the third question, the Hon'ble Court held that it is only when the Tribunal comes to the conclusion that any of the measures, referred to in Section 13(4), taken by the secured creditor that are not in accordance with the provisions of the Act and the Rules made there under, only then can the Tribunal restore possession of such secured assets to the borrower. The statutory scheme of the SARFAESI Act is such that the borrower could take recourse to application under Section 17 only if one or other measure is taken by the secured creditor, and the Tribunal can restore the status quo ante only if it comes to the conclusion that any of the measures taken by the secured creditor were not in accordance with the provisions of the Act.

Regarding the fourth question, the Hon'ble Court held that Section 17 of the SARFAESI Act provides remedy for the borrower/guarantor/mortgagor to challenge the action of the bank under Section 13(4) of the Act before the Debt Recovery Tribunal. The Debt Recovery Tribunal is required to decide whether the action of the bank/financial institutions, under Section 13(4), is in accordance with the provisions of the Act and the Rules framed there under. It is open to the borrower/guarantor/mortgagor to demonstrate before the Debt Recovery Tribunal that a resort to Section 13 of the Act is not permissible by law. In a given case, the claim of the bank/financial institutions may be barred by limitation or there may be cases where the adjustment of the amount paid is not reflected in the notice or the calculation of interest may not be in accordance with the contract between the parties. Needless to say that all such grounds, which render the action of the bank/financial institutions illegal, can be raised in the proceedings under Section 17 of the Act before the Debt Recovery Tribunal. It is for the Debt Recovery Tribunal to decide in each case whether the action of the bank/financial institution was in accordance with the provisions of the said Act and legally sustainable.

IX. *Kottakkal Co-operative Urban Bank v. T. Balakrishnan & Others*

The Hon'ble Kerala High Court has held in *Kottakkal Co-operative Urban Bank v. T. Balakrishnan & Others*[13] that it would always be well within the wisdom and freedom of the secured creditor to determine in any given case if he should exercise the authority of u/s 13(4) and take over de jure and de facto possession all at once or whether he should let the secured debtor continue to hold de facto possession after taking over only de jure possession. It is not a requirement of Section 13(6) or any of the other provisions of the Act that a transfer by a secured creditor after taking over possession could be only after taking over actual possession de facto. The right to take possession invoking the provisions u/s 13(4) (a) is provided in such wide terms that it gives fair room for the secured creditor to decide whether it would first proceed only to take de jure possession.

The petitioner in this case, Kottakkal Co-operative Urban Bank, initiated proceedings under the Securitisation and Reconstruction of Financial Assets and Enforcement of Security Interest Act, 2002, against the respondent and took what can be called "symbolic possession" of the property but left the respondent in de facto physical possession. The property was later brought for sale, and a sale certificate was issued in favour of the auction purchaser. Thereafter the petitioner moved the petition u/s 14(I) of the SARFAESI Act before the learned chief judicial magistrate. The learned chief judicial magistrate dismissed the aforesaid petition as not maintainable on the grounds that the petitioner had already taken possession, effected a sale and issued a sale certificate; therefore, there was no need to take possession by invoking the powers of u/s 14 of the Act.

The Hon'ble High Court held that what Section 13(4)(a) authorises is to take possession of the secured assets of the borrower, including the right to transfer by way of lease, assignment or sale for releasing the secured asset. A close reading of the relevant sections showed that there is no stipulation in Section 13 or elsewhere that the right to transfer can be exercised only after taking over the actual physical possession or that the exercise of taking over possession u/s 13(4) shall be of actual physical possession, resulting in the complete dispossession of the secured debtor, de facto and de jure.

The Hon'ble Court further held that while there is a vesting of rights, exclusively with the transferee under a sale in terms of Section 13(6), such vesting of sale gives the transferee the right to demand of the secured creditor actual physical possession. Such deemed vesting, by operation of law, gives the entitlement to the transferee to insist that the secured creditor puts the transferee in de facto possession by dispossessing the secured debtor who continues in de facto possession only by the choice of the secured creditor to take only de jure possession, leaving the secured debtor with actual possession. Therefore, the secured creditor, who has taken de jure possession, continues to be a secured creditor, duty bound to give the transferee de facto possession, and such liability of the secured creditor gives sufficient standing to sustain the application for the dispossession of the secured creditor of de facto possession over the security interest by recourse to Section 14 of the Act. The results of that proceeding would be that the secured debtor would be dispossessed of actual possession, and de facto possession would be taken by the secured creditor, who would then, duty bound as he is, transfer such de facto possession to the transferee of rights under Section 13(6) of the Act.

The Hon'ble High Court set aside the order of the learned chief judicial magistrate and further directed that the learned chief judicial magistrate would take back the application filed u/s 14(1) of the SARFAESI Act and proceed with the same in accordance with the law.

X. *Kamal Gupta and etc. v. Bank of India and Another*

The issue which came up for adjudication before the Hon'ble Court in *Kamal Gupta and etc. v. Bank of India and Another*[14] is in regard to the exact and intended meaning of the word "borrower" as defined under Section 2(f) read with Section 13(2) of the SARFAESI Act. The Hon'ble Court held that upon examination of the definition of the term borrower in Section 2(f), keeping in mind the provisions of Section 13 of the SARFAESI Act, it is clear that the word borrower will include the person who created any mortgage or pledge as well as his legal representatives. Keeping in mind the objective and purpose of the Act, it cannot be said that legal representatives should be excluded from the word borrower. The relationship between the borrower and the bank or the financial institution is created by contract under the Indian Contract Act, 1872. The promise made by the promisor is binding on his representatives in case of his/her death, unless a contrary intention appears in the contract. The promise to perform an obligation under contract is not personal to the contracting party, but it is also binding on his representatives. The legal representatives are, under law, liable for the debts of their predecessor to the extent of any property inherited by them from their predecessor in interest. The legal representatives are not personally liable for the liability, but the liability is to the extent of the estate of the deceased inherited by them.

In this case, one Smt. Parvati Devi stood as a guarantor for the financial assistance granted to M/s ROM Industries Ltd. by Bank of India. On 19th August 2000, Smt. Parvati Devi passed away and left behind her legal heirs. Thereafter, the Bank of India filed a recovery application before the DRT in respect of the aforesaid loan and also issued notice under Section 13(2) of the SARFAESI Act to the legal representatives of Smt. Parvati Devi. The said notice under the SARFAESI Act was challenged before the learned single judge of the High Court by filing three separate writ petitions which were dismissed by the learned single judge by holding that under the definition in Clause 2(f), a borrower would mean the principal borrower and after his or her death, it would be his/her legal representatives. Aggrieved by the said order, the legal representatives of Smt. Parvati Devi filed an instant appeal.

The Hon'ble Division Bench of the High Court found no merit in their appeals and dismissed the same by holding that the legal representatives and legal heirs of Smt. Parvati Devi would also be liable, and their liability was not absolved on her death. The Hon'ble Court further held that Section 59A of the Transfer of Property Act, 1882, clarifies that references to the mortgagor and mortgagee would include persons deriving the title from them.

A conjoined reading of the provisions of the Contract Act, Transfer of Property Act and SARFAESI Act makes it clear that the word "borrower" as defined in Section 2(f) of the SARFAESI Act would mean the original borrower and, after his or her death, his/her legal representatives. The legal representatives' step into the shoes of the predecessor on the title who had mortgaged the property.

XI. *Standard Chartered Bank v. Applitech Solution Ltd & Others*

Securitisation, in essence, is the financing or refinancing of income yielding assets by packaging them into a tradable form through the issue of bonds or other securities. A securitisation or reconstruction company comes in between the secured creditor and the borrower and pays the secured creditor the value of his loan at a discount and thereafter deals with the borrower directly on the basis of securities recovered from the secured creditor, relieving the secured creditor from resorting to a recovery process against its borrowers. As a result of securitisation, the securitisation and reconstruction company steps into the shoes of the secured creditor. The Securitisation and Reconstruction of Financial Assets and Enforcement of Security Interest Act (SARFAESI Act) was enacted to facilitate the securitisation and reconstruction of financial assets and the enforcement of security interest in the year 2002. Section 5 of the SARFAESI Act is an enabling provision, which provides for the acquisition of the financial assets of any banks or financial institution by any securitisation company or reconstruction company. The Division Bench of the Gujarat High Court held in *Standard Chartered Bank v. Applitech Solution Ltd & Others*[15] that where the rights and liabilities of a bank are assigned in favour of another bank, the assignee can always prosecute the proceedings before the Debt Recovery Tribunal. In this case, the ICICI Bank assigned the rights and liabilities from the consent decree in favour of Standard Chartered Bank. The Division Bench of the High Court observed that both ICICI Bank as well as Standard Chartered Bank would fall with the definition of a "banking company" under Section 2(e) of the Recovery of Debts Due to Banks and Financial Institutions Act, 1993, and shall have the meaning assigned to it in Clause (C) of Section 5 of the Banking Regulation Act, 1949.

In the aforementioned case, ICICI Bank received a consent decree from the Debt Recovery Tribunal and upon default of the respondent in making payment in terms of the consent decree, ICICI Bank filed an application for the execution of a recovery certificate. ICICI Bank later, through a deed of assignment with the Standard Chartered Bank, assigned the rights and liabilities of the respondent, Applitech Solution Ltd, along with various other companies. Pursuant to the deed of assignment, Standard Chartered Bank filed a civil mis. application before the DRT, seeking the substitution of Standard

Chartered Bank in place of ICICI Bank Ltd at nine places in the recovery certificate. The application was opposed by the respondents stating that once a recovery certificate was issued, the same couldn't be rectified or corrected. However, the Hon'ble Court held that where the rights and liabilities of a bank are assigned in favour of another bank, the assignee can always prosecute the proceedings before the Debt Recovery Tribunal.

XII. *Ram Murty Pyara Lal and Others v. Central Bank of India and Others*

The legal issues pertaining to the rights of the mortgagor to redeem the mortgage *vis-à-vis* Section 13(8) of the SARFAESI Act came up for consideration before the Hon'ble DRAT in M/s. *Ram Murty Pyara Lal and Others v. Central Bank of India and Others.*[16] In this case, the property of the appellants had been sold by the mortgagee-bank to the auction purchaser under the provisions of the SARFAESI Act, and after confirmation of the sale, the sale certificate was also issued. The aggrieved appellants submitted before the Hon'ble DRAT that the right of redemption is an incidence of subsisting mortgage, and it cannot be denied till the right of redemption is extinguished legally; hence the mortgagor has a right to redeem the mortgage even after the issuance of a sale certificate. The Hon'ble DRT dismissed the application filed by the borrower. Thereafter, the borrowers approached DRAT. The Hon'ble DRAT and observed that the SARFAESI Act has been enacted to empower the banks/financial institutions to take possession of the securities and to sell them without the intervention of court. The Section 13(8) of the SARFAESI Act provides that if the dues of the secured creditor together with all costs, charges and expenses incurred by him are tendered to the secured creditor at any time before the date fixed for sale or transfer, the secured asset shall not be sold or transferred by the secured creditor and no further step shall be taken by him for transfer or sale of that secured asset. Hence, the Hon'ble DRAT held that the right of redemption of mortgage can be exercised before the sale of property and not thereafter.

XIII. *J. Malliga and Others v. Authorized Officer, Union Bank of India, Regional Office, Madurai, (2010) 4 MLJ*

The moot legal question that arose in a batch of writ petitions[17] before the Madurai bench of the Madras High Court was regarding the construction of the words "agricultural land" found in Section 31(i) of the Securitisation and Reconstruction of Financial Assets and Enforcement of Security Interest Act (SARFAESI), 2002. The Hon'ble Court held that the loan was sanctioned for cardamon planting and the cultivation of the cardamom requires normal agricultural activities. Hence, the bank cannot proceed against the properties of the petitioners under the SARFAESI Act as the subject land is agricultural land.

According to the borrowers/petitioners, the lands, which were given as collateral security to the respondents, are cardamom plantations, and the impugned notice issued by the authorised officer of the bank clearly refers to the word "cardamom plantation"; therefore, without any further investigation, it would be logical to conclude that they are agricultural lands, and hence, they are immune from attachment. The respondent bank submitted that without evidence to show that such land had been cleared and prepared or earmarked for agricultural purposes, it must be treated as prima facie non-agricultural land.

The Hon'ble High Court refer to various decisions of the Hon'ble Supreme Court of India such as the decision in *W.T. Commr., A.P v. Court of Wards,* Paigah AIR 1977 SC, wherein the Hon'ble Supreme Court observed that the term "agriculture" for the purpose of Indian Income-Tax Act meant some measure of cultivation of the land and some expenditure of skill and labour upon it, and if the operations, whether they be agricultural operations or forestry operations, did not conform with those definitions, they could not be styled agricultural operations.

The Hon'ble High Court held that applying the normal principles of interpretation in fiscal statures, if there are two views possible, the one favourable to the assessee should be given. In this case, the one that was favourable to the petitioners, who are the borrowers, should be given. In the present case, it is admitted that it is a cardamom estate, and the loan was sanctioned for new cardamon planting, and the cultivation of the cardamom requires normal agricultural activities.

In view of the aforementioned, the Hon'ble Court held that the notice issued under Section 13(2) of the SARFAESI Act is without jurisdiction, and the respondent bank cannot proceed against the properties of the petitioners under the SARFAESI Act. However, the Hon'ble Court was specific in noting that the respondent bank has the right to recover the amounts due in a manner known to law, and the invocation of the SARFAESI Act alone is held to be barred by Section 31(i) of the SARFAESI Act.

XIV. *Omeshwar Baldwa v. Vasavi Co-operative Urban Bank Ltd*

While dealing with the writ petition between *Omeshwar Baldwa v. Vasavi Co-operative Urban Bank Ltd*[18] that was challenging the legality and validity of the notice issued by the respondent bank in terms of Section 13(2) of the SARFAESI Act, the division bench of the Hon'ble Andhrapradesh High Court held that there is nothing wrong with invoking the provision contained under Section 13(2) and 13(4) even after there has been a lapse of time since the asset has been declared a non-performing asset.

The writ petitioner availed themselves of a term loan facility from the respondent bank but defaulted in repaying the dues. On 21 June 2004, the respondent bank issued notice under Section 13(2) of the SARFAESI Act and called upon the writ petitioner to liquidate the dues within 60 days from the receipt of the notice. The writ petitioner did not respond to the said notice. The writ petitioner submitted before the Hon'ble Court that once a notice is issued under Section 13(2) of the SARFAESI Act, the bank has no choice but to proceed further in the matter and carry the same to its logical end. Since the respondent bank issued such a notice on 21 June 2004, but failed to carry the same any further, it cannot now issue another notice under Section 13(2), after a lapse of nearly 5 years. After careful analysis of the provisions of the SARFAESI Act, the Hon'ble High Court held that the secured creditor is at liberty to take recourse to one or more of the measures in the process of recovering the debt. When a stature has provided for various options to be explored by a creditor, it is not liable to be inferred that one of them or all of them in the same serial order as they are specified in the enactment should be explored inevitably. When the SARFAESI Act has not provided any further time limits for the period of time that the steps or measures enumerated under Section 13(4) must be accomplished, it is not open for the court to construe a time limit for accomplishing the said objectives. The Hon'ble Court further held that what the statute intends is that no steps contemplated by Section 13(4) are liable to be taken first without a notice under Section 13(2) is issued.

XV. *Cham Trading Organisation and Others v. Authorised Officer and Chief Manager Bank of Baroda, Ahmedabad*

The legal validity of the proceedings initiated by the bank in pursuance of the notice issued under Section 13(2) of the SARFAESI Act and which was later found defective came for consideration before the Hon'ble DRAT, Mumbai in M/s. *Cham Trading Organisation and others v. Authorised Officer and Chief Manager Bank of Baroda, Ahmedabad.*[19]

The appellant borrowers were granted credit facilities by the respondent bank. Their accounts were declared NPAs. Notice under Section 13(2) of the SARFAESI Act was issued to the appellant borrowers. The appellant borrowers replied to the notice, and the respondent bank considered the reply and admitted that the amount claimed in the notice was without giving a credit of Rs.2,01,90,000. The amount claimed in the notice was revised, and a communication was sent to the appellant borrowers.

Thereafter the respondent bank issued a possession notice and took symbolic possession of the secured assets. Aggrieved against the action of the respondent bank, the appellant borrower filed a securitisation application and contended that there was no compliance of Rule 3A (b) of the Security Interest Enforcement Rules and asked for the quashment of notice. The respondent bank defended its action under the SARFAESI Act. The Debt Recovery Tribunal came to the conclusion that admittedly, the amount deposited Rs.2.01 crores were not reflected in the demand notice. However, the respondent bank corrected the said mistake in its reply, after considering the representation of the applicants. Therefore, the contention that there can be no further proceedings based on such a defective notice cannot be accepted at this stage.

Aggrieved against the DRT order, the appellant borrowers approached DRAT. The Hon'ble DRAT held that a plain reading of the provisions makes it clear that in cases of changes or modifications in the demand notice, the same shall be modified accordingly, and a revised notice shall be served upon the borrower. However, in this case, the modified demand notice was not served upon the appellants. The Hon'ble DRAT held that since, in the case on hand, no revised notice was served upon the appellants, the subsequent action of the service of notice under Rule 8(1) of the rules is not in accordance with law. Therefore, the action taken by the respondent bank subsequent to the reply cannot be said to be according to law and cannot be upheld. Accordingly, the Hon'ble DRAT set aside the actions of the respondent subsequent to the notice and directed the respondent bank to serve the modified notice under Section 13(2) of the SARFAESI Act to the appellant borrower and proceed in the matter according to law.

XVI. *Jupiter Jewel Tech represented by Its Partners & Others v. Authorised Officer, Indian Overseas Bank, Chennai*

In this case,[20] the petitioner is a partnership firm and took a cash credit limit from the respondent bank. The respondent bank issued a notice under Section13(2) of the SARFAESI Act. The petitioners gave a reply, which was apparently rejected by the authorised officer. Thereafter, the bank took steps under Section 13(4) of the SARFAESI Act by issuing a notice regarding taking possession. Subsequently, the petitioners filed S.A. no.84 of 2008 before the Debt Recovery Tribunal challenging the action purportedly taken under Section 13(4) of the SARFAESI Act. The main contention that was raised before the DRT relates to the illegality of the reply given by the authorised officer. It is submitted that having himself issued a notice under Section 13(2) of the SARFAESI Act, the objection/reply filed by the petitioners under Section 13(2) of the SARFAESI Act should have been considered by the secured creditor and not by the very same authorised officer.

The Hon'ble High Court observed that Rule 3-A of the Security Interest Enforcement Rules, 2002, which relates to the question of the disposal of the petition/representation made by the borrower is obviously pursuant to the observation made in the *Mardia Chemicals Ltd v. Union of India* case, which resulted in the introduction of Section 13 (3-A) and Rule 3-A. The three sub-clauses in Rule 3-A are to be considered as different facets of the same aspect, namely the reply to the representation of the borrower.

The Sub-Clause (a) of Rule 3-A imposes a duty on the authorised officer to consider the representation or objection on examining whether the same is acceptable or tenable. The Sub-Clause (b) of Rule 3-A contemplates that if, upon examining the representation, it is felt that there is a need for any modification, it shall be made, and the revised notice may be issued, or other suitable orders may be passed within 7 days from the date of the representation or objection. The Sub-Clause (c) of Rule 3-A contemplates that on examining the representation or objection if it is not acceptable, he shall communicate the reasons for non-acceptance within 1 week. The two clauses only reflect two sides of same coin, namely the duty to consider the representation or objection as insisted by the Supreme Court in *Mardia Chemicals Ltd v. Union of India* and incorporated in the Act and rules in the shape of Section 13(3-A) and Rule 3-A. If the objection is acceptable, the necessary correction is required to be made within 1 week, and if the objection is not acceptable, the reasons for non-acceptance are to be indicated to the borrower within 7 days.

Therefore, in the context in which Rule 3-A has been incorporated, it must mean that the officer who is required to consider the representation and take suitable action either in rectifying the mistakes, if any, or communicating the reasons for non-acceptance of the representation may be one and the same. Any other meaning would make the provision unworkable. Merely because a person issues a notice, one cannot assume the person is biased. If such a view is accepted, it would mean that in service jurisprudence relating to disciplinary proceedings, the disciplinary authority who frames charges and seeks explanations would be considered a biased authority and consequently should not take any decision. If such a contention is accepted, it may make the Act and Rules unworkable. It is for the secured creditor to take its own administrative decision as to whether the person who is issuing notice should also be the officer dealing with the reply. In view of the aforementioned findings, the Hon'ble Court held that the contention raised by the petitioner is not acceptable, and accordingly the civil revision petition was dismissed.

XVII. *Saraspathy Sundararaj Proprietrix v. The Authorised Officer and Assistant General Manager, State Bank of India, SARB, Chennai*

The Division Bench of the Hon'ble High Court of Madras held in *Saraspathy Sundararaj Proprietrix v. The Authorised Officer and Assistant General Manager, State Bank of India, SARB, Chennai*[21] that a writ petition challenging the possession notice after a lapse of 6 years is not maintainable. A brief description of the factual matrix of the case is provided here:

The petitioner, who is the borrower of the Stressed Assets Recovery Branch (SARB), Chennai of the respondent bank, committed default in repayment of the loan. Consequently, the borrower's account was classified as a NPA as per the directions of the RBI with respect to the Income Recognition and Asset Classification. The SARB of the respondent branch issued notices under Section 13(2) of the SARFAESI Act. Thereafter the respondent bank took possession of the mortgaged properties of the petitioner by issuing a possession notice under Section 13(4) of the SARFAESI Act.

The petitioner approached the Hon'ble High Court asking for a writ of certiorarified mandamus calling for the records relating to the possession notice issued under the SARFAESI Act against the petitioner and to quash the same and direct the respondent to effect the settlement in accordance with the SBI OTS-SME 2010 scheme and unconditionally restore physical possession of the mortgaged properties.

The Hon'ble Court held that the possession notice sent to the petitioner way back in the year 2004 remained unchallenged till 2010 when she approached the competent forum, namely the Debts Recovery Tribunal. When a specific forum was created which enables the borrower to challenge the action of the financial institution by filing the necessary petition under Section 17, the petitioner is not entitled to invoke the writ jurisdiction of this court. The Hon'ble Court further held that the decision to dismiss the writ petition is fortified by the decision of the Hon'ble Supreme Court reported in *United Bank of India v. Satyawati Tandon and Others*, wherein the Hon'ble Supreme Court held that the High Courts must exercise discretion with great caution, care and circumspection while passing orders which have a serious adverse impact on the rights of banks and other financial institutions to recover their dues.

A brief analysis of the other important judgements is presented next:

The Hon'ble Supreme Court held in *Kotak Mahindra Bank Ltd.*[22] *v. Dilip Bhosale* that when a remedy under the statute is available and was availed upon by the respondent/borrower, a filing of a writ petition under Article 226 of the Constitution is to be discouraged by the High Court.

In *Phoenix ARC Private Limited v. Vishwa Bharati Vidya Mandir & Others*,[23] the Hon'ble Supreme Court held that a writ petition against the private financial institution – ARC – appellant herein under Article 226 of the Constitution of India against the proposed action/actions under Section 13(4) of the SARFAESI Act can be said to be not maintainable. In the present case, the ARC proposed to take action/actions under the SARFAESI Act to recover the borrowed amount as a secured creditor. The ARC as such cannot be said to be performing public functions which are normally expected to be performed by the state authorities. During the course of a commercial transaction and under the contract, the bank/ARC lent the money to the borrowers herein and therefore the said activity of the bank/ARC cannot be said to be as performing a public function which is normally expected to be performed by the state authorities. If proceedings are initiated under the SARFAESI Act and/or any proposed action is to be taken and the borrower is aggrieved by any of the actions of the private bank/bank/ARC, the borrower has to avail themselves of the remedy under the SARFAESI Act, and no writ petition would lie and/or is maintainable and/or entertainable.

In the case of *Tirupati Storage and Allied Pvt Ltd. v. the United Commercial Bank, Kolkata*, reported in 2012 (4) PLJR 748, the Patna High Court considered the issue under Section 13(2) in the SARFAESI Act in para 15 of the judgement and specifically held that by using the word "details" before the expression "of the amount payable", the Legislature clearly intended that in the notice under Sub-Section 2, the details of the calculation of principal and interest must be mentioned. In the case of *Madhu Sudan Ghosh & Others v. the Bank of Baroda & Others*, reported in MANU/WB/0349/2010, of the High Court of Calcutta, the court, on appreciating the provisions of Section 13(2), specifically held that the notice under Section 13(2) shall give details of the amount payable.

The Delhi High Court has held in *Kanu Aditya India Ltd v. SBI* that merely because the requirement of a secured creditor to consider a representation or an objection raised by the borrower has been held to be mandatory, it doesn't necessarily mean that the period within which the lender must respond as specified under Section 13 (3A) is also to be construed to be mandatory. The intention of Parliament in providing a time period of 15 days was to ensure that the secured creditors respond within reasonable time, and hence the said period is directory in nature.

XVIII. *Bajarang Shyamsunder Agarwal v. Central Bank of India & Another*[24]

The Hon'ble Supreme Court held that the objective of the SARFAESI Act, coupled with the TP Act and the Rent Act are required to be reconciled herein in the following manner:

(1) If a valid tenancy under law is in existence even prior to the creation of the mortgage, the tenant's possession cannot be disturbed by the secured creditor by taking possession of the property. The lease has to be determined in accordance with Section 111 of the TP Act for the determination of leases. As the existence of a prior existing lease inevitably affects the risk undertaken by the bank while providing the loan, it is expected of banks/creditors to have conducted a standard due diligence in this regard. Where the bank has proceeded to accept such a property as mortgage, it will be presumed that it has consented to the risk that comes as a consequence of the existing tenancy. In such a situation, the rights of a rightful tenant cannot be compromised under the SARFAESI Act proceedings.

(2) If a tenancy under law comes into existence after the creation of a mortgage, but prior to the issuance of notice under Section 13(2) of the SARFAESI Act, it has to satisfy the conditions of Section 65A of the TP Act.

(3) In any case, if any of the tenant's claim that he is entitled to possession of a secured asset for a term of more than a year, it has to be supported by the execution of a registered instrument. In the absence of a registered instrument, if the tenant relies on an unregistered instrument or an oral agreement accompanied by delivery of possession, the tenant is not entitled to possession of the secured asset for more than the period prescribed under Section 107 of the TP Act.

XIX. *Harshad Govardhan Sondagar v. International Assets Reconstruction Co. Ltd & Others*[25]

The Hon'ble Supreme Court held that when action is sought to be taken by the secured creditor under Section 13 of the SARFAESI Act or by the CMM or DM under Section 14 of SARFAESI Act, the court or the authority in the Rent Control Act can't grant an injunction to prevent such action by the secured creditor or by the CMM or DM.

If any of the appellant's claims are that they are entitled to possession of a secured asset for any term exceeding 1 year from the date of the lease made in his favour, he has to produce proof of execution of a registered instrument in his favour by the lessor. Where he doesn't produce proof of execution of a registered instrument in his favour and instead relies on an unregistered instrument or oral agreement accompanied by delivery of possession, the CMM or DM will come to the conclusion that he is not entitled to the possession of the secured asset for more than a year from the date of the instrument or from the date of delivery of possession in his favour by the landlord.

The CMM or DM will consider the claims of the appellants that they were in possession of the secured asset under a lease made prior to the creation of the mortgage and decide the applications under Section 14 in accordance with this judgement and any other law that may be relevant after giving the opportunity of a hearing to the appellants and the secured creditors.

XX. *Vishal N. Kalsaria v. Bank of India & Others*[26]

The Hon'ble Supreme Court held that the decision of Supreme Court rendered in the case of Harshad Govardhan Sondagar cannot be understood to have held that the provisions of the SARFAESI Act override the provisions of the Rent Control Act and that the banks are at liberty to evict the tenants residing in the tenanted premises which have been offered as collateral securities for loans on which a default has been made by the debtor/landlord.

When granting leasehold rights created after the property has been mortgaged to the bank, the consent of the creditor needs to be obtained. This view was taken in the case of Harshad Govardhan Sondagar. But there is no statement to the effect that the tenancy created after mortgaging the property must necessarily be registered under the provisions of the Registration Act and the

Stamp Act. It is a settled position of law that once tenancy is created, a tenant can be evicted only after following the due process of law, as prescribed under the provisions of the Rent Control Act. A tenant cannot be arbitrarily evicted by using the provisions of the SARFAESI Act as that would amount to stultifying the statutory rights of protection given to the tenant. A non obstante clause (Section 35 of the SARFAESI Act) cannot be used to bulldoze the statutory rights vested on the tenants under the Rent Control Act.

In view of the aforementioned legal position, the SC held that if we accept the legal submissions made on behalf of the banks to hold that the provisions of SARFAESI Act override the provisions of the various Rent Control Acts to allow a bank to evict a tenant from the tenanted premise, which became a secured asset of the bank after the default on the loan by the landlord, and dispense with the procedure laid down under the provisions of the various Rent Control Acts and the law laid down by this court in a catena of cases, then the legislative powers of the state legislatures are denuded, which would amount to subverting the law enacted by the state legislature. Surely, such a situation was not contemplated by Parliament while enacting the SARFAESI Act, and therefore the interpretation sought to be made by the learned counsel appearing on behalf of the banks cannot be accepted by this court as the same is wholly untenable in law.

In view of this, the impugned judgements and orders passed by the High Court/chief metropolitan magistrate are set aside, and the appeals are allowed. The court further directed that the amounts which were in deposit pursuant to the conditional interim order of this court towards rent either before the chief metropolitan magistrate/magistrate court or with the concerned banks, should be adjusted by the concerned banks towards the debt due from the debtors/landlords in respect of the appellants in these appeals. The enhanced rent by way of a conditional interim order should be continued to be paid to the respective banks, and the amount shall also be adjusted towards debts of the debtors/landlords. All the pending applications were disposed of.

XXI. *R.D. Jain and Co. Versus Capital First Ltd. & Ors.*

CIVIL APPELLATE JURISDICTION
CIVIL APPEAL NO. 175 OF 2022

The Hon'ble Supreme Court held that the district magistrate or chief metropolitan magistrate is not a persona designata for the purposes of Section 14 of the SARFAESI Act. The terms "district magistrate" and "chief metropolitan magistrate" as appearing in Section 14 of the SARFAESI Act were deemed to mean and include the additional district magistrate and the additional chief metropolitan magistrate for the purposes of Section 14 of the SARFAESI Act.

Thus, the Hon'ble Supreme Court held that the judicial powers, and the powers under the Cr. PC which may be exercised by the chief metropolitan magistrate, can be exercised by the additional chief metropolitan magistrate also. Thus, the additional chief metropolitan magistrate can be said to be on par with the chief metropolitan magistrate in so far as the powers to be exercised under the Cr. PC are concerned.

XXII. *S.K. Bakshi Vs. Punjab National Bank*

WP(C) No. 465/2021
CM No. 4507/2021

The Hon'ble High Court held that the respondent bank categorically mentioned in the notice as well as in the sale certificate stated that the property is free from all encumbrances; therefore, the respondent bank was bound to deliver the physical possession of the property to the purchaser. The property was not delivered to the petitioner, despite paying a huge amount in the auction; rather the entire auction proceedings lost their value and came to naught. Although the physical possession of the property did not need to be taken before being put to auction, the respondents cannot shirk from their duty to hand over the physical possession of the property to the auction purchaser. If respondent no. 1 was not in a position to take the physical possession of the same before the sale, then they had to adopt a course under Section 14 of the Act. The contention of respondent no. 1 that there is no statutory obligation on their part to put the auction purchaser in possession thus does not hold any merit. Ordinarily, the sale would be complete when the receipt of the entire sale consideration and the possession was handed over, but if there were encumbrances mentioned in the sale certificate or in the auction, then it could be argued that the petitioner had entered into an agreement knowing this fact and had purchased the property and taken the risk which came with it. But in the present case, it was specifically mentioned in the sale certificate that there was no encumbrance in the property; the petitioner could not be expected to know that the property was already in use by some persons. It was the responsibility of respondent no. 1 to specify the known encumbrance attached to the property, and having failed to do so, the respondent bank is duty bound to provide the physical possession of the property to the petitioner.

XXIII. *L and T Finance Ltd V/s. State of Maharashtra*

WRIT PETITION NO. 15285 OF 2022

The Hon'ble High Court directed that till the state government set a procedure as mentioned earlier, if any secured creditor has a grievance with an order passed by the district magistrate that is not being complied with, the district magistrate will give audience to the representative of the secured creditor and proceed to give instructions or pass orders as may be warranted in law and fact. The district magistrate is expected to take administrative action against the officers who are not following or implementing the order of the district magistrate without legal reason. If the secured creditor has a grievance that, in spite of all compliances, Section 14 of the SARFAESI Act is not decided by the district magistrate within 60 days, it will be open to the secured creditor to approach the divisional commissioner with a representation who will look into the representation and issue necessary instructions.

XXIV. *Surinder Pal Singh V/s. Vijaya Bank*

CIVIL APPEAL NO.6843 OF 2023 (ARISING FROM SLP (C) NO.16771/2018)

The Hon'ble Supreme Court held that the right of the borrower to redeem would be available till the sale certificate is registered and the possession is handed over, after which the borrower will not have a right for redemption under the unamended provision of Section 13 (8) of the SARFAESI Act.

XXV. *S. Karthik & Ors. V/s. N. Subhash Chand Jain & Ors.*

Supreme Court of India Civil Appellate Jurisdiction-CIVIL APPEAL NO S. 5920–5923/2021

The Hon'ble Supreme Court held that the SARFAESI Act was enacted with the purpose for securitisation and to empower banks and financial institutions to take possession of the securities and to sell them without the intervention of the court. If we look at the facts in the present case, it shows that every attempt was made to frustrate the purpose of the SARFAESI Act. The respondent bank was required to indulge in three rounds of litigations, and the two finally reached this court. In that view of the matter, the Hon'ble Court did not find any merit insofar as the challenge to the SARFAESI notice by the borrower.

XXVI. *K. Sreedhar V/s. M/s. Raus Construction Pvt. Ltd.*

CIVIL APPEAL NOS. 7402 OF 2022 (@ SLP (Civil) No. 14695 of 2020)

The Hon'ble Supreme Court held that the High Court materially erred in shifting the burden upon the secured creditor to prove that the properties were not non-agricultural lands or have been put to non-agricultural use. When it was the case on behalf of the borrowers that in view of Section 31(i) of the SARFAESI Act, the properties were agricultural lands and were exempted from the provisions of the SARFAESI Act, the burden was upon the borrower to prove that the secured properties were agricultural lands and actually being used as agricultural lands and/or agricultural activities were going on. Therefore, the High Court materially erred in shifting the burden upon the secured creditor to prove that the properties are non-agricultural lands or have been put to non-agricultural use.

XXVII. *M/s. Sama Rubbers V/s. South Indian Bank Ltd.*

OP (DRT) NO. 392 OF 2023

The Hon'ble High Court held that the inquiry conducted by the chief judicial magistrate under Section 14 of the SARFAESI Act does not result in an adjudication of the parties inter se rights regarding the subject matter. It is an administrative or executive function regarding the verification of the affidavit and documents relied on by the parties. The authority must display a judicial approach in considering the relevant facts asserted by the parties. It is a quasi-judicial inquiry through a non-judicial process.

XXVIII. *NKGSB Cooperative Bank Ltd., Subir Chakravarty & Ors.*

CIVIL APPEAL NO............... OF 2022 (@ S.L.P. (CIVIL) NO.30240 OF 2019)

The Hon'ble Supreme Court held that we are persuaded to take the view that Sub-Section (1A) of Section 14 of the 2002 Act is no impediment for the CMM/DM to engage services of an advocate (an officer of the court) – only for taking possession of secured assets and documents relating thereto and to forward the same to the secured creditor in furtherance of the orders passed by the CMM/DM under Section 14(1) of the 2002 Act in that regard. It does not follow that the advocate so appointed needs to be on the rolls in the office of the CMM/DM or in public service. There is an intrinsic *de jure* functional subordinate relationship between the CMM/DM and the advocate being an officer of the court. The apprehension of the borrowers about the improper execution of orders of the CMM/DM passed under Section 14(1) of the 2002 Act by the advocate commissioner is plainly misplaced. Further, being an officer of the court and appointed by the CMM/DM, the acts done by an advocate commissioner would receive immunity under Section 14(3) of the 2002 Act, as an officer authorised by the CMM/DM. There is no reason to assume that the advocate so appointed by the CMM/DM would misuse the task entrusted to him/her and that it will not be carried out strictly as per law; otherwise, it would be a case of an abuse of power. Rather, going by the institutional faith or trust reposed on advocates being officers of the court, there must be a presumption that if an advocate is appointed as commissioner for execution of the orders passed by the CMM/DM under Section 14(1) of the 2002 Act, that responsibility and duty will be discharged honestly and in accordance with rules of law.

XXIX. *Kotak Mahindra Bank Pvt. Ltd V/s. Ambuj A. Kasliwal & Ors.*

CIVIL APPEAL NO. 538 OF 2021

The Hon'ble Supreme Court held that when a further amount is due and payable in discharge of the decree/recovery certificate issued by the DRT in favour of the appellant/bank, the High Court does not have the power to waive the pre-deposit in its entirety, nor can it exercise discretion that is against the mandatory requirement of the statutory provision as contained in Section 21 of the SARFAESI Act. In all cases, 50% of the decretal amount, i.e. the debt due, is to be deposited before the DRAT as a mandatory requirement, but in appropriate cases for reasons to be recorded, a deposit of at least 25% of the debt due would be permissible, but not an entire waiver. Therefore, any waiver of pre-deposit to the entire extent would be against the statutory provisions and, therefore, not sustainable in law. The order of the High Court is, therefore, liable to be set aside.

XXX. *K. Virupaksha & Anr. . . . Appellant(s) Versus The State of Karnataka & Anr. . . . Respondent(s)*

CRIMINAL APPELLATE JURISDICTION
CRIMINAL APPEAL NO. 377 OF 2020
(Arising out of SLP (Criminal) No.5701 of 2019)

The Hon'ble Court held that Section 32 of the SARFAESI Act provides immunity from prosecution for action taken in good faith. A criminal proceeding would not be sustainable in a matter of the present nature and exposing the appellants bank officials to the proceedings before the investigating officer or the criminal court would not be justified.

XXXI. *Kotak Mahindra Bank Ltd V/s. Dilip Bhosale*

Special Leave to Appeal (C) No(s). 13241–13242/2019
Supreme Court of India

The Hon'ble Supreme Court observed that this court is consistent in the view, as seen in the judgement in *United Bank of India v. Satyawati Tandon & Others*, that when a remedy under the statute is available and, in this case was indeed availed by the respondent/borrower, filing of a writ petition under Article 226 of the Constitution is to be discouraged by the High Court. Consequently, the special leave petitions in the light of the aforementioned observations are dismissed as having become infructuous.

Conclusion

In view of the analysis of the case laws as discussed in this chapter, it can be concluded that the judgements of the various High Courts and the Supreme Court have contributed heavily to the development of the laws relating to the recovery of dues. In fact, these judgements have paved the way in clarifying the doubts that arose in the implementation of the laws. These judgements have fortified and strengthened the foundation of the recovery laws and also led to guidance on the growth of recovery laws in our jurisprudence.

****

Notes

1 Mardia Chemicals Ltd v. Union of India & Others, reported in 2004 D.R.T.C 1(SC).
2 Transcore v. Union of India and Another, reported in AIR 2007 SC 712, MANU/SC/5319/2006.
3 Collector of Customs, Madras v. Nathella Sampathu reported in 1962(3) SCR 786 at pp. 829–830.
4 Kishanchand Arora v. Commissioner of Police reported in 1961(3) SCR 135.
5 Transcore v. Union of India and Another, AIR 2007 SC 712, MANU/SC/5319/2006.
6 Authorised Officer, Indian Overseas Bank v. Ashok Saw Mill reported in 2009(2) D.R.T.C.545 (SC).
7 Civil Appeal – SLP© No.10145 of 2010, United Bank of India v. Satyawati Tondon and Others.
8 City and Industrial Development Corporation v. Dosu Aardeshir Bhiwandiwala and Others, (2009) 1 SCC 168.
9 Eureka Forbes Limited v. Allahabad Bank and Other, Civil Appeal No.4029 of 2010 (Arising out of SLP © No.3883 of 2008).
10 Indian Bank v. Blue Jaggers Estates Ltd and Others reported in 2010(4) Current Tamil Nadu Cases (SC).
11 ICICI Bank v. Shanti Devi Sharma and Others, 2008(2) Bank CLR 745 (SC).
12 M/s. Lakshmi Shankar Mills (P) Ltd. & Others v. Authorised Officer/Chief Manager, Indian Bank & Others, etc. (Reported in AIR 2008 Madras 181).
13 Kottakkal Co-operative Urban Bank v. T. Balakrishnan & Others, AIR 2008 Kerala 179.
14 Kamal Gupta and etc. v. Bank of India and Another, 2008(2) Bank CLR 369 (Del).
15 Standard Chartered Bank v. Applitech Solution Ltd & Others, AIR 2009 Gujarat 54.
16 M/s. Ram Murty Pyara Lal and Others v. Central Bank of India and Others, 2010(1) Bank CLR 70 (DRAT Del).
17 J. Malliga and Others v. Authorized Officer, Union Bank of India, Regional Office, Madurai, (2010) 4 MLJ.

18 Omeshwar Baldwa v. Vasavi Co-operative Urban Bank Ltd, 2010(1) Bank CLR 680 (AP).
19 M/s. Cham Trading Organisation and Others v. Authorised Officer and Chief Manager Bank of Baroda, Ahmedabad, 2010(1) Bank CLR 594 (DRAT Mum).
20 Jupiter Jewel Tech represented by Its Partners & Others v. Authorised Officer, Indian Overseas Bank, Chennai, 2010(1) D.R.C.714 (Mad).
21 Mrs. Saraspathy Sundararaj Proprietrix v. The Authorised Officer and Assistant General Manager, State Bank of India, SARB, Chennai, CDJ 2010 MHC 5284-W.P. No. 15146 of 2010 & M.P. No. 1 of 2010.
22 Special Leave to Appeal (C) No(s). 13241–13242/2019 Kotak Mahindra Bank Limited Petitioner(s) v. Dilip Bhosale Respondent(s).
23 Civil Appeal Nos. 257–259 of 2022 Phoenix ARC Private Limited v. Vishwa Bharati Vidya Mandir & Others.
24 Bajarang Syamsunder Agarwal v. Central Bank of India & Another, AIR 2019 Supreme Court 5017.
25 Sondagar v. International Assets Reconstruction Co. Ltd & Others, Criminal Appeal No.736/14 S.L.P (Crl.) No.1666/12.
26 Vishal N. Kalsaria v. Bank of India & Others, AIR 2016 Supreme Court 530.

Chapter 6

The issues and challenges in enforcing the SARFAESI Act, 2002

Although the SARFAESI Act was an enabling act for the banks to recover their dues from the default borrowers without approaching the court of law, the hardships and difficulties imposed on the genuine borrowers/borrowers can't be ignored. Many of the borrowers/guarantors call the SARFAESI Act a draconian act enacted only for the benefit of the banks. Some of the provisions of the SARFAESI Act have been criticised on many counts from different quarters. An analysis of the various challenges faced by the stakeholders while implementing the SARFAESI Act is explored next for a better understanding.

I. The provisions of the SARFAESI Act shall be subject to the state tenancy laws

The rights of the tenants of the property which has been possessed by the authorised officer of the bank have come up for consideration before the Hon'ble High Court of Madras in *Indian Bank v. M/s. Nippon Enterprises South*.[1]

In the aforementioned case, M/s. Elke Enterprises had availed certain financial facilities from the bank, and the financial facilities were secured by the equitable mortgage created over the immovable properties belonging to Mr. Shyam Narain and Mr. Bharat Shyam Narain. M/s. Elke Enterprises committed default in repayment of the financial facilities, and therefore the bank invoked the provisions of the Securitisation and Reconstruction of Financial Assets and Enforcement of Security Interest Act, 2002. Aggrieved by the action of the authorised officer, the tenant filed W.P. No. 17337 of 2009 seeking an order prohibiting the bank from taking possession of the property. The contention of the tenant was that their right to continue to be in possession of the property in question as a lessee is protected by the Tamilnadu Rent Control Act. It was further contended that the SARFAESI Act cannot extinguish the right accrued to a tenant under the provisions of the TN Rent Control Act. The contention of the bank was that the SARFAESI Act has an overriding effect over the TN Rent Control Act in view of the

DOI: 10.4324/9781003546238-6

provisions of Section 35, and therefore the rights said to have been accrued in favour of the tenant under the TN Rent Control Act cannot be enforced against the bank while the bank invokes the provisions of the SARFAESI Act.

After hearing both of the parties, the Hon'ble High Court held that if Parliament intended to give priority to the dues of banks, financial institutions and other secured creditors over the first charge created under state legislations, then a similar provision would have been incorporated in the SARFAESI Act. Further, there is no provision in the SARFAESI Act in respect to taking possession from the hands of the tenant. But the right of the tenant to continue to be in possession is protected by the TN Rent Control Act. The SARFAESI Act is an act for the expeditious recovery of dues to the banks, financial institutions and secured creditors, whereas the purpose of the TN Rent Control Act is to protect the possessions of the tenants. The High Court was of the view that the bank cannot take physical possession from the tenant protected under the TN Rent Control Act by invoking the provisions of Sections 13(4) and 14 of the SARFAESI Act, in the event the tenant is in a bona fide occupation.

In *Harshad Govardhan Sondagar v. International Assets Reconstruction Co. Ltd & Others*,[2] the Hon'ble Supreme Court held that the secured creditor cannot take possession of the mortgaged property where the lessee is in possession under a valid registered lease deed executed by the mortgagor prior to the creation of the mortgage, until the same is expired. Hence, wherever the lessee is in possession of secured asset, the bank can't take possession by dispossessing the mortgagor.

II. The authorised officer is not acting in good faith and fair play

Many have raised doubts regarding the neutral position of the authorised officer while discharging his duties under the SARFAESI Act. The secured creditor is initiating the proceedings through his representative, i.e. the authorised officer. It is being criticised that the authorised officer takes the role of a prosecutor for the recovery of the bank's dues and later acts as a quasi-judicial authority. The authorised officer is an employee of the secured creditor, and he is under its disciplinary and administrative control. In these given circumstances, it may not be possible for him to act independently and give a reasonable quasi-judicial decision. In practice, the authorised officer represents the interest of the secured creditor, and the entire role he plays is that of an enforcement officer/prosecuting officer. Many of the experts recommend that the mode of functionality of an authorised officer under this Act has to be reviewed and changed.

In practice, when representations or objections are made, it is found that almost all the authorised officers make flat denials and reject the objections or representations of the notice/borrower without giving any proper reasons for rejecting them. The borrower is clueless and not properly informed of the details of the claim. There is a necessity to hold that the authorised officer must give all the grounds for the contemplated action under Section 13(2) of the Act. Without giving a proper disclosure of claim and documents in support of the claim, the borrower has no reasonable opportunity to understand the claim.

The Act is treating willful defaulters and non-willful defaulters on the same footing, and drastic powers of enforcement are equally applied to both. In countries like the United States, there is the Lenders Liability Act. However, there is no such legislation in India, and the SARFAESI Act having the one-sided protective measure in favour of secured creditors clearly violates the human conscience and sense of justice. Many criticise that legislation such as the SARFAESI Act makes Shylock, the rich man, a saint.

III. The publication of the photograph of the borrower/guarantor

The question of whether the authorised officer of a bank is empowered to publish the photograph of the borrower/guarantor is discussed by the High Court of Bombay in *D.J. Exim (India) Pvt. & Others v. State Bank of India & Others*.[3] The Hon'ble High Court held that a perusal of the Enforcement of Security Interest Rules, 2002, clearly indicates that the bank has the right to publish the name of the defaulters by giving their names and addresses, and a twofold purpose is served as a result of the said publication of the names. Firstly, the fact that these persons are willful defaulters is made known to the public at large, and secondly it also cautions the prospective buyers who may be offered the property which is mortgaged by these defaulters with the bank. This is the primary objective for the publication of the notice; there would be no impediment in the publication of photographs of willful defaulters and particularly those defaulters who have committed various acts of misfeasance. There is no legal bar either in the said rule or under any provisions of the Act which expressly prohibits the bank from publishing photographs, and therefore the action of the bank in publishing the photographs cannot be held to be *ultra vires*. However, it appears that the right of privacy available to the borrowers/guarantors have not been considered and found place in the judgement.

IV. Chief judicial magistrates have the power to issue orders under Section 14 of the SARFAESI Act

Taking possession of the secured assets under Section 13 of the SARFAESI Act is an integral part of the SARFAESI proceedings. In order to enable the authorised officers to take possession of the secured asset, a provision has been made under Section 14 of the SARFAESI Act to approach the chief metropolitan magistrate or district magistrate.

In the plain interpretation of Section 14, the chief metropolitan magistrate or district magistrate is empowered to assist the authorised officer of the bank to take possession of the secured assets. The question of whether or not the chief judicial magistrate can also exercise the powers given under Section 14 of the SARFAESI Act was discussed by the High Court of Madras in 2009 in *Indian Overseas Bank v. Sree Aravindh Steels Ltd.*[4] The Hon'ble Court held that the chief metropolitan magistrate will have jurisdiction in metropolitan areas and in non-metropolitan areas, and beside the district magistrate, the power can also be exercised by the chief judicial magistrate. The Hon'ble High Court of Kerala in *Muhammed Asharaf v. Union of India*[5] held that the chief judicial magistrate can also exercise the powers under Section 14 of the SARFAESI Act.

However, the Hon'ble High Court of Madras (Madurai Bench) in *K. Arockiyaraj v. The Chief Judicial Magistrate, Srivilliputhur, Virudhunagar District*[6] held that Section 14 of the SARFAESI Act does contemplate that the secured creditor will approach the chief judicial magistrates for assistance in securing their assets. The secured creditors can approach the chief metropolitan magistrate in metropolitan areas, and in non-metropolitan areas, the secured creditor has to approach the district magistrate and not the chief judicial magistrate. However, the Hon'ble Supreme Court of India settled this issue in M/s. *R.D. Jain and Co. v. Capital First Ltd. & Others*[7] and held that the powers under Section 14 of the SARFAESI Act can be exercised by the concerned additional chief metropolitan magistrates that have jurisdiction and by the additional district magistrates, who otherwise are exercising the powers at par with the concerned district magistrates either by delegation and/or special order.

V. Civil court does not have jurisdiction

Section 34 of the Securitisation Act ousts the civil court jurisdiction. For easy reference, we may extract Section 34 of the Securitisation Act, which is as follow:

> 34. Civil Court not to have jurisdiction – No civil court shall have jurisdiction to entertain any suit or proceeding in respect of any matter which a Debts Recovery Tribunal or the Appellate Tribunal is empowered by or under this Act to determine and no injunction shall be granted by any court or other authority in respect of any action taken or to be taken in pursuance of any power conferred by or under this Act or under the Recovery of Debts Due to Banks and Financial Institutions Act, 1993.

However, we can see that in a good number of cases that are in the realm of the DRT for adjudication are being entertained by civil courts, and stay orders are also being issued restraining the further proceedings under the SARFAESI Act. In this context, the judgement of the Hon'ble Supreme Court of India in *Jagdish Singh vs. Heeralal and Others*[8] is important. The Hon'ble Supreme Court held that the civil court jurisdiction is completely barred, so far as the "measure" taken by a secured creditor under Sub-Section (4) of Section 13 of the Securitisation Act, against which an aggrieved person has a right of appeal before the DRT or the Appellate Tribunal. The Tribunal is to determine if there has been any illegality in the "measures" taken by the secured creditor.

VI. Whether the bank (secured creditor) is entitled to proceed simultaneously under the DRT Act and the SARFAESI Act

The single judge of the High Court of Patna held in M/s. *Purnea Cold Storage v. SBI, Authorised Officer, SAMB, Patna*[9] that the bank is not entitled to approach the Debt Recovery Tribunal under the provisions of the Recovery of Debt Due to Banks and Financial Institutions Act (RDDBFI Act) 1993 without exhausting the remedies available under the SARFAESI Act.

While allowing an appeal against the order of the single judge, the division bench of the Patna High Court held that there is nothing in the provisions of the SARFAESI Act or the RDDBFI Act to suggest that the invocation of one would forbid the invocation of the provisions contained in the other. The Hon'ble Court also discussed the judgement of Supreme Court in M/s. *Transcore v. Union of India & Another*,[10] wherein it is stated that withdrawal of OA before the DRT was not a condition precedent for invoking the SARFAESI Act. The Hon'ble Court further observed that if securitisation is permissible during the pendency of the recovery proceedings under the RDDBFI Act, there is no reason why the recovery proceedings would become legally bad just because the bank had taken resort to Securitisation Act. What is important is that both the proceedings can be instituted and maintained simultaneously. If that were so, just because the proceedings under the Securitisation Act had been instituted earlier, it would not render the proceedings before the DRT bad. The fact that there is a period of limitation prescribed for filing the suit before the DRT also makes it necessary for the banks and financial institutions to institute such suits within the period of limitations stipulated for the same. Any delay in doing so would jeopardise the maintainability of such suits, which banking institutions cannot afford to risk, especially where the amounts outstanding against the borrowers are huge.

VII. Whether the authorised officer can approach the CMM or DM before making an attempt to take possession of the property by issuing Section 13(4) of the Act

The question of whether the authorised officer can approach the CMM or DM before making an attempt to take possession of the property by issuing Section 13(4) of the Act was examined by the Hon'ble Supreme Court in *Standard Chartered Bank v. Noble Kumar & Others*.[11] The Hon'ble Court held that there would be three methods for the secured creditor to take possession of the secured assets:

i. The first method would be where the secured creditor gives the requisite notice under rule 8(1) and where he does not meet with any resistance. In that case, the authorized officer will proceed to take steps as stipulated under rule 8(2) onwards to take possession and thereafter for sale of the secured assets to realize the amounts that are claimed by the secured creditor.
ii. The second situation will arise where the secured creditor meets with resistance from the borrower after the notice under rule 8(1) is given. In that case, he will take recourse to the mechanism provided under section 14 of the Act viz. making application to the Magistrate. The Magistrate will scrutinize the application as provided in section 14 and then, if satisfied, appoint an officer subordinate to him as provided under section 14 (1) (A) to take possession of the assets and documents. For that purpose, the Magistrate may authorize the officer concerned to use such force as may be necessary. After the possession is taken the assets and documents will be forwarded to the secured creditor.
iii. The third situation will be one where the secured creditor approaches the Magistrate concerned directly under section 14 of the Act. The Magistrate will thereafter scrutinize the application as provided in section 14 and then if satisfied, authorize a subordinate officer to take possession of the assets and documents and forwards them to the secured creditor as under clause (ii) above.

VIII. Delay in disposal of an application filed under Section 14 of the SARFAESI Act

One important problem which cropped up during the implementation of the SARFAESI Act is the delay that occurred in the disposal of the application filed under Section 14 of the SARFAESI Act. In this context, the judgement delivered by the division bench of the Hon'ble High Court of Bombay in *International Asset Reconstruction Company Private Ltd v. Union of India and Others*[12] is important in settling down the guidelines in this regard. The Hon'ble Court has held that banks and financial institutions deal with public money, and it is in the interest of general public to see that they take possession of the secured assets and recover money advanced by them where the borrower is under liability and his account has become non-performing.

IX. Legal validity of e-auction under the SARFAESI Act

The Hon'ble High Court of Madras in its judgement in *M/s. Kanchee Fashion Sarees & Others v. Authorised Officer, SBI, Kancheepuram & Others*, dated 20 February 2014, upheld the legal validity of the e-auction sale notices issued by some of the authorised officers of the banks. While dismissing the writ petitions challenging the legal validity of the e-auction notices, the Hon'ble High Court observed that there is no specific prohibition, either under the Securitisation and Reconstruction of Financial Assets and Enforcement of Security Interest Act, 2002, or under the Security Interest (Enforcement) Rules, 2002, restraining the respondent banks and the authorities concerned from employing the e-auction sale process, for the sale of the secured assets. There is no doubt that the banks have chosen to adopt the method of e-auction sale, for selling the properties in question, with the bona fide intention of obtaining the best possible price for the said properties. Thus, it is clear that the e-auction sale procedures followed by the respondent banks would only be beneficial to the owners of the properties in question and the banks concerned, which are the secured creditors.

X. Whether a subsequent sale notice required the compliance of all the provisions enumerated in Rules 8 and 9(1)

The issue of whether a subsequent sale notice was required to comply with all the provisions under Rules 8 and Rule 9 of the Security Interest (Enforcement) Rules, 2002, was discussed by the two bench judges of the Hon'ble Supreme Court in *Mathew Varghese v. M. Amritha Kumar and Others.*[13] The Hon'ble Court held that unless and until a clear 30-day notice is given to the borrower, no sale or transfer can be completed by a secured creditor. In the event of any such sale properly notified after giving a 30-day clear notice to the borrower that did not take place as scheduled for reasons which cannot be solely attributable to the borrower, the secured creditor cannot affect the sale or transfer of the secured asset on any subsequent date by relying upon the notification issued earlier. In other words, once the sale does not take place pursuant to a notice issued under Rules 8 and 9, read along with Section 13(8), it is imperative that for effecting the sale, the procedure provided in the rules must be followed afresh, as the notice issued earlier would lapse. Now rule 9 of the Security Interest (Enforcement) Rules, 2002 has been amended to incorporate a provision, which state that for subsequent sale, 15 days sale notice is sufficient.

XI. Banks are not following the RBI guidelines on the SARFAESI Act

It is reported that[14] in their hurry to recover unpaid loans, banks seem to be ignoring the basic rules of the game. The borrowers allege that the recovery notices are devoid of detailed information and proper authorisation. A notice under the Securitisation and Reconstruction of Financial Assets and Enforcement of Security Interest Act allows banks to liquidate the mortgaged/hypothecated assets of borrowers after a notice of 60 days. The Act, however, also allows borrowers to raise objections to the notice, and it is incumbent on the bank to respond to those objections within 15 days. Many borrowers are unaware of this right. In most cases, the banks, which ask borrowers to repay the dues within 60 days, did not mention their right to raise objections to the notice.

XII. Whether the consent of borrower is required to conduct the sale of the property by private treaty

The issue of whether the consent of the borrower is required to conduct the sale of the property by private treaty was discussed by the Hon'ble Supreme Court in *J. Rajiv Subramaniyan & Another v. M/s. Pandiyas & Others.*[15] The Hon'ble Supreme Court held that there were no terms settled in writing between the parties that the sale can be affected by private treaty. In fact, the borrowers were not even called to the joint meeting between the bank and recovery agent. Therefore, there was a clear violation of the rules which rendered the sale illegal. The Hon'ble Court held that the creditor should ensure that the borrower was clearly put on notice of the date and time by which either the sale or transfer would be effected in order to provide the required opportunity for the borrower to take all possible steps to retrieve his property. Such a notice is also necessary to ensure that the process of sale will ensure the secured assets will be sold to provide maximum benefit to the borrowers. Subsequent to this judgment, rule 8 of the Security Interest (Enforcement) Rules, 2002 was amended to include sub-rule 8, which state that sale by any methods other than public auction or public tender shall be on such terms as may be settled between the secured creditor and the proposed purchaser in writing.

Conclusion

The important points from the discussion in this chapter reveal that the provisions of the SARFAESI Act and the DRT Act face a lot of challenges and problems at the level of enforcement. The discussion exposed the inner deficiencies and inherent problems of both acts. The intensity and the complication of the problems faced at the level of implementation of the DRT and SARFAESI Acts have compelled the successive governments at the Centre to appoint various committees to find solutions for the smooth working of these acts. The identification and fixation of the problems will help in formulating necessary schemes for the eradication of these issues by making necessary amendments in the acts and also making necessary policies for the successful implementation of these acts.

Notes

1 Indian Bank v. M/s. Nippon Enterprises South, AIR 2011 Madras 230.
2 Harshad Govardhan Sondagar v. International Assets Reconstruction Co. Ltd & Others, Criminal Appeal No.736 of 2014.
3 D.J. Exim (India) Pvt. Ltd & Others v. State Bank of India & Others, Writ Petition (L) No.2808 of 2013.
4 Indian Overseas Bank v. Sree Aravindh Steels Ltd, 2009(1) CTC 341 (DB).
5 Muhammed Asharaf v. Union of India, AIR 2009 Ker 14.
6 K. Arockiyaraj v. The Chief Judicial Magistrate, Srivilliputhur, Virudhunagar District, 2013(5) CTC 15.
7 M/s. R.D. Jain and Co. v. Capital First Ltd & Others, Civil Appeal No.175/2022.
8 Jagdish Singh v. Heeralal, Civil Appeal No.9771/2013 (Arising out of Special Leave Petition (Civil) No.18 of 2011).
9 M/s. Purnea Cold Storage v. State Bank of India, Authorised Officer, SAMB, Patna C.W.J.C. No.8746 of 2012.
10 M/s. Transcore v. Union of India & Another, AIR 2007 SC 712.
11 Standard Chartered Bank v. Noble Kumar & Others, Criminal Appeal No.1218 of 2013.
12 International Asset Reconstruction Company Private Ltd v. Union of India and Others, Crl. Public Interest Litigation No.24 of 2011.
13 Mathew Varghese v. M. Amritha Kumar and Others, MANU/SC/0114/2014, Civil Appeal Nos.1927–1929 of 2014.
14 *The Business Line* – Published on 13 March 2014; article by Satyanarayan Iyer entitled "In a hurry to recover loans, Banks ignore the rules of the game – Recovery notices slapped on borrowers lack detailed information, proper authorization".
15 J. Rajiv Subramaniyan & Another v. M/s. Pandiyas & Others, Civil Appeal No.3866/2014, S.L.P© No.25448/2012.
M/s. Kanchee Fashion Sarees & Others v. Authorised Officer, SBI, Kancheepuram & Others, dated 20 February 2014.

Chapter 7

The Insolvency and Bankruptcy Code, 2016

A big game changer in banking!

The introduction of the IBC was considered to be the most powerful weapon in the hands of the bankers to reduce the frightening level of non-performance assets. It is expected that the IBC will change the game plan of NPA management in the Indian banking space. The main objectives of the code were time-bound reorganisation, maximisation of value of assets, promotion of entrepreneurship, availability of credit and balanced interests of all stakeholders.

The euphoria around the IBC may prompt many to ask whether the IBC is a big game changer in the banking space *vis-à-vis* the previous recovery laws such as civil courts, the DRT Act and the SARFAESI Act. Prior to the IBC, the Indian banking space was dominated by legal measures such as civil courts, the DRT Act and the SARFAESI Act. These measures have been extensively used by Indian bankers to bring down the levels of NPAs.

I. Comparative analysis of the IBC, the SARFAESI Act, the DRT and civil courts

Though the IBC, the SARFAESI Act, the DRT and the civil courts have their own uniqueness in enabling bankers to recover their dues, an attempt is made here to do a comparative analysis by touching upon the core fundamental competitiveness of the aforementioned acts.

1. IBC – Paradigm shift from 'debtor-in-possession' to 'creditor-in-control'

The biggest advantage of the IBC is the paradigm shift in taking possession of the assets from the corporate debtor to the creditors. This behavioural change has caused a phenomenon change in the prescription of the borrowers towards recovery laws. The IBC has changed the debtor-creditor relationship: the creditor no longer chases the debtor; those who drive the companies to insolvency exit from management.

DOI: 10.4324/9781003546238-7

2. *IBC – Recognises the spirit of entrepreneurship*

India is one of the youngest republics in the world, with a high concentration of the most dynamic entrepreneurs. The IBC may be the first act which recognises the spirit of entrepreneurship. The economy of any country shall flourish only if it recognises the spirit of entrepreneurship. The contribution of Silicon Valley to the growth of United States is immense and laudable. It is not surprising that most of the tech companies that rule the world today started their journeys in Silicon Valley.

In fact, the Sick Industrial Companies Act (SICA) and the Board for Industrial and Financial Reconstruction (BIFR) have been formulated to treat the liquidation of assets of a business only after it has lost all of its value. In stark contrast to such an approach, the IBC has been formulated to treat the business of borrowing as an ongoing concern. The IBC envisaged a business continuity concept. The concept of moratorium was introduced to enable the smooth transition of business. By rescuing viable businesses and closing non-viable ones, the Code releases the entrepreneurs from failure. It enables them to get in and get out of business with ease, undeterred by failure.

3. *IBC – Recognises a judicial hands-off*

It is a judicially accepted norm that in the matter of economic legislation, courts will interfere only if it is absolutely necessary. The IBC has recognised the concept of a judicial hands-off, which means less judicial interference. In the IBC, it is interesting to understand that the judiciary wing under IBC, i.e. the adjudicating authority, has no role to play in the approval or rejection of a resolution plan. It is purely a financial decision to be taken by financial creditors. The role of the judiciary is limited to judicial adjudication and not on credit-related matters.

4. *IBC – Recognises the dominant role of creditors*

The concept of crown debts and its priority over bankers' rights have been debated for long in banking circle. The bankers fought several rounds of litigation with government/tax authorities for their priority rights. It was a relief for bankers when the IBC recognised their priority rights over government dues. Although Section 31B of the Recovery of Debts and Bankruptcy Act and Section 26E of the SARFAESI Act accorded the right of priority to bankers over government dues vide amendment made on 1 September 2016, we have yet to witness substantial progress in this regard. However, the IBC has accorded not only priority rights to bankers but also accorded a low priority to government dues in specific terms – unlike the Companies Act, 2013, where government dues were being paid alongside employees and unsecured financial creditors. Now, government dues are paid after secured creditors, unsecured creditors, employees and workmen. The IBC viewed the government only as a facilitator and regulator and not as an active participant in the affairs of commercial entities.

5. *IBC – Expediting decision-making process*

The credit decisions to be made by banks under the IBC were instantaneous compared to the time-consuming decisions bankers used to make during previous regimes. Going by the level of hierarchy in the public sector banks, making an instantaneous decision is quite difficult. However, even the public sector banks were forced to take quick decisions in view of the risk of deterioration in the value of the assets of borrower companies. However, it is amazing to see that even public sector banks have lived up to expectations and are delivering decisions within the given time frame of the IBC.

The Code endeavours for a resolution of insolvency at the earliest time, preferably at the very first default, to prevent it from ballooning to un-resolvable proportions. In early days of default, enterprise value is typically higher than the liquidation value, and hence the stakeholders would be motivated to resolve the insolvency of the firm rather than liquidate it. Therefore, it entitles the stakeholders to initiate the Corporate Insolvency Resolution Process (CIRP) as soon as there is threshold amount of default.

6. *IBC – Time is the essence*

The Code mandates resolution in a time-bound manner, as undue delay is likely to reduce the enterprise value of the firm. When the firm is not in sound financial health, prolonged uncertainty about its ownership and control may make the possibility of resolution remote. Time is the essence for the Code. It provides a mandatory timeline of 180 days for the Committee of Creditors (CoC) to conclude CIRP, extendable by a one-time extension of up to 90 days.

One of the biggest challenges with respect to the litigation in India is the uncertainty over the time period for the disposal of cases. Although both DRT/SARFAESI proceedings stipulated a time limit for the disposal of appeals/applications, it seldom happens. The failure to comply with the time limit is reflected in the majority of the cases. It appears that the time-bound resolution process under the IBC is more realistic. The IBC recognises that speed is the essence of its proceedings.

7. *IBC – No more stay orders*

In the previous recovery regime, the borrowers/guarantors could obtain stay orders frequently and continued to remain in possession on the strength of stay orders for a long period of time. However, under the IBC, borrowers/guarantors are finding it difficult to obtain stay orders, and even if it is obtained, it is short lived. The borrowers/guarantors realised that there was no way out from losing control of businesses on the admission of the application.

8. *IBC – Option to select better and more efficient managers*

Under the IBC, the financial creditors were given liberty to select better and more efficient managers to run the debtor company, which is in stark contrast to previous regimes where the same borrower who has failed on multiple occasions has been given further chances to run the company. The Sick Industrial Companies (Special Provisions) Act, 1985, which made provisions for the rehabilitation of sick companies and the repayment of loans availed by them, was found to have completely failed.

9. *IBC – Separation of powers between commercial and judicial domains*

The IBC separates commercial aspects of insolvency and bankruptcy proceedings from judicial aspects. Under the IBC, the adjudicatory authority has been given only powers to pass judicial decisions and not on credit decisions. The financial creditors have been given absolute freedom to accept or reject a resolution application.

The civil court/DRT/SARFAESI envisaged a judicial-centric proceeding that left a little role for other stakeholders. However, under the IBC, important roles have been provided to financial creditors, operational creditors, and corporate debtors. Under DRT/SARFAESI, the courts control the entire process of resolution/recovery, leaving no scope for decision-making by stakeholders. The failure is being penalised under the previous regime apart from prescribing cumbersome legal proceedings.

The Code segregates commercial aspects of insolvency resolution from judicial aspects and empowers the stakeholders and adjudicating authority to decide matters within their respective domain expeditiously. It puts the entire process at the disposal of the stakeholders and motivates them with incentives and disincentives to complete the process at the earliest time possible. The commercial decisions of the CoC are not generally open to any analysis, evaluation or judicial review by the adjudicating authority or the appellate authority.

10. *IBC – More realistic approach*

It is unrealistic to believe that all business enterprises will succeed, generate income, and earn profit. Many business enterprises ought to fail due to factors which are beyond one's own control. So, a more realistic approach would be to admit business failures and formulate a legal framework to provide a quick solution to such failures. The previous recovery laws concentrate their attention more on the recovery of debts rather than the reorganisation or restructure of business enterprises.

The IBC has envisaged a more realistic approach towards the revival of the business units. It envisaged a mechanism whereby the management of the firm and its assets vest in an insolvency professional (IP), who runs the firm as a going concern, and a CoC (Committee of Creditors) is constituted to evaluate options for the firm. The IP invites feasible and viable resolution plans from eligible and credible resolution applicants for the resolution of insolvency of the firm. If the CoC approves a resolution plan within the stipulated time with a 66% majority, the firm continues as a going concern. If the CoC does not approve a resolution plan with the required majority within this period, the firm mandatorily undergoes liquidation.

The Code makes an attempt, by divesting the erstwhile management of its powers and vesting it in a professional, to continue the business of the firm as a going concern until a resolution plan is drawn up. Then the management is handed over under the plan so that the firm can pay back its debts and get back on its feet. All this is done within a period of 6 months with a one-time extension of up to 90 days or else the liquidation process begins.

11. IBC – Going concern concept

The Code envisages resolution of the firm as a going concern, as the closure of the firm destroys organisational capital and renders resources idle till reallocation to alternate uses, which make the possibility of resolution remote. It, therefore, facilitates continued operation of the firm as a going concern during CIRP, which is a paradigm shift from the previous recovery laws. It makes available a cadre of competent and empowered IPs to manage the affairs of the firm under the resolution as a going concern, to protect and preserve the value of its property, help in retrieval of value lost through fraudulent and preferential transactions and assist the CoC to arrive at the best resolution plan. In previous recovery regimes, the concepts of going concern and a person to manage the affairs of the ailing company or firm were absent.

To ensure the smooth management of the corporate debtor, the IBC mandates the firm, its promoters, and any other person associated with its management to extend all assistance and cooperation to the IP. It envisages information utilities to make available authentic information required for completing the process expeditiously. It enables raising interim finances and includes the cost of interim finance in the insolvency resolution process cost, which has super priority. It envisages a moratorium on the institution and a continuation of suits or proceedings against the firm during the resolution period. It prohibits the suspension or termination of the supply of essential services to the firm to keep it going. It prohibits any action to foreclose, recover, or enforce any security interest during CIRP and thereby prevents a creditor(s) from maximising its individual interest. So, altogether, the IBC provides a different experience from the previous recovery laws. The IBC values entrepreneurship, while previous regimes looked at the default company/firm as merely a physical asset for recovery only.

12. *IBC – Instils a better sense of credit discipline*

The IBC has instilled a better sense of credit discipline as there is a sense of urgency and seriousness among defaulting borrowers because losing their asset is a possibility if the resolution process fails. This is reflected in the slower accretion of new non-performing assets (or bad loans) in the Indian banking system. As per RBI report,[1] the gross non-performing assets (GNPA) and net NPA (NNPA) ratios continued to decline and stood at 7.5% and 2.1%, respectively, in September 2020.

13. *IBC – Projects a team effort*

There are many players that have defined, complementary roles to complete the process. It is a team responsibility to complete the process in time, although one person has the prime responsibility for a task in the process. The IBC doesn't envisage an adversarial system of proceedings. There is no pleading or defending party, and the terminologies like petitioner, respondent, plaintiff and defendant are not present under the Code. However, in previous recovery regimes, a team effort was absent, and it was a legal fight between bankers on the one hand and borrowers/guarantors on the other hand.

The IBC balances the interests of stakeholders in the resolution process. It aims to balance the interests of all stakeholders and does not maximise value for financial creditors (FC). Since it does not envisage recovery during CIRP, it does not provide for a waterfall in distribution of the recovered amount among the creditors, as it provides the order of priority for distribution of proceeds from sale of liquidation assets. It, however, incorporates the principle of fair and equitable dealing for the rights of all stakeholders.

14. *Role of Resolution Professional*

Under the IBC, the resolution professional plays an important role. Under the SARFAESI Act and the DRT, there was no role for a resolution professional. At the most, receivers were appointed to take custody of the assets of the borrowers/guarantors, but the role of such receivers was limited. They were not given the power to prepare a resolution plan or liquidate the borrower company.

15. The IBC v. the DRT/SARFEASI/LOK ADALAT – recovery in real terms

The Economic Survey 2020–21 pointed out that the recovery of non-performing assets of scheduled commercial banks was highest under the Insolvency and Bankruptcy Code compared to other debt recovery methods. The survey said IBC recoveries were more than the combined recoveries each year under Lok Adalat, Debt Recovery Tribunal and the SARFAESI Act.

As per the Crisil data reported in May 2019, the recovery through the IBC was at Rs.70,000 crore and twice the Rs.35,000 crore recovered through previous resolution mechanisms like the DRT, the SARFAESI Act and Lok Adalat.

Conclusion

It is true to state that the IBC has matured over the last 8 years. The IBC ecosystem has been developed over the period of time and now comprises 16 benches of AA, 2500 and more IPs, 3 insolvency professional agencies, 50 insolvency professional entities, 1 information utility, 1200 registered valuers and 11 registered valuer organisations. The judicial forums like AA, the NCLAT and the courts have been very active in implementing of the Code. The Supreme Court, High Courts and National Company Law Tribunals have settled several critical legal issues and brought clarify to the roles of the various stakeholders in the resolution process. It appears that the IBC is going to be the largest body of case laws.

The government has demonstrated its leadership role in insolvency reforms. RBI has pushed very large corporates with very high NPAs into resolution process. The proactive efforts of RBI to clean up the banks' NPAs have also achieved reasonable result. Although the judgement of the Hon'ble Supreme Court declaring the RBI circular issued on 12 February 2018 as ultra vires of Section 35AA of the Banking Regulation Act[2] has posed serious legal issues, the underlying fact is that the constitutional validity of the IBC has been upheld by the Supreme Court.

The IBC has enabled India to record a big jump of 23 positions in its rank of 100 in 2017 in the Ease of Doing Business Index. Now India stands at the rank of 63 among 190 countries assessed by the World Bank.[3]

However, the IBC has a long way to go in ensuring the smooth functioning of the resolution of corporate debts. In 2016, an insolvency resolution in India took 4.3 years on an average, while it took 1 year in United Kingdom and 2 years in South Africa. The large burden on the National Company Law Tribunal to resolve large number of cases, clarity on the priority of claims, a limited number of information utilities and the creation of a secondary asset market need to be addressed. The IBC ecosystem is indeed strengthening at a fast pace. Going ahead, success will hinge on timely resolutions of stressed assets and a conducive system. The IBBI's proactive stance in seeking and acting on feedback from stakeholders' is going well, as testified by the fact that the IBC has undergone two major amendments already.

We may state that the IBC is an evolving legislation, which has shown results in last 8 years, especially in comparison to the erstwhile recovery and distress resolution framework. The IBC reinvigorated a stressed asset space with strategic as well as financial investors being bullish about the prospects of investment.

Though the IBC proved a potential weapon in the fight against stressed assets, it is not to a one-time solution for all issues in the banking recovery space. There is a need to strengthen the other recovery mechanisms along with the IBC. The IBC has taken within its fold large corporate resolutions, and it was able to show progress in terms, volume and capacity. However, other recovery mechanisms such as the DRT, the SARFAESI Act, civil court and Lok Adalat have their own roles to play in debt resolution. There is equally a need to strengthen other recovery laws along with the IBC. Hopefully in coming days, the IBC, along with other recovery measures, will rejuvenate the banking recovery space in India and bring more recovery to reduce the level of non-performing assets.

Notes

1 RBI report dated 11 January 2021 – Chapter II: Financial Institutions: Soundness and Resilience.
2 Dharani Sugars and Chemicals Ltd v. Union of India & Others, Transferred Case (Civil) No.66/2018.
3 Press released by Ministry of Commerce & Industry dated 31 October 2019.

Chapter 8

Implications of the SARFAESI Act on various systems

The laws relating to the recovery of dues to banks and financial institutions, especially the SARFAESI Act, have passed through various stages of its evolution. These Acts have also subjected to various judicial scrutiny from different judicial forums and have faced stiff legal obstacles. In its long journeys, the recovery laws, both DRT and the SARFAESI Act, have proved to be beneficial legislations in facilitating the recovery of large dues to the banks, albeit with attentive delay, unavoidable litigation and instances of misuse and arbitrary use of powers by authorised officers of the banks. The redressal mechanism as provided under the SARFAESI Act hasn't been able to solve the difficulties faced by the borrowers and guarantors while implementing the provisions of the Act.

It is no doubt that the Recovery of Debts Due to Banks and Financial Institutions and the Securitisation and Reconstruction of Financial Assets and Enforcement of Security Interest Act have had a tremendous effect on the jurisprudence relating to the laws governing the recovery of dues to the banks. However, as time evolves, the inherent deficiencies in these Acts have come for adjudication before various judicial forums. The issues sprung from the practical difficulties faced by the borrowers and guarantors have reached judicial forum at various occasions.

Notwithstanding the interference of judicial forums in shaping the recovery laws, it is equally important to note the established stand taken by the highest courts in our country regarding the maximum restraint in economic legislation. The judicial system in our country is sensitive to the issue that less judicial interference is required in economic legislations. This is true in cases of the laws pertaining to the recovery of dues to the banks/financial institutions. The judicial system in our country, even the highest court of the country, the Supreme Court, kept maximum restraint in interfering with the provisions of the SARFAESI Act. The economic mechanism is highly sensitive and complex and primarily such legislations are directed to solve practical problems. Most of the economic problems are singular and contingent,

DOI: 10.4324/9781003546238-8

and the economic laws addressing such problems are not abstract propositions, do not relate to abstract units and are not to be measured by abstract symmetry. The economic matters are essentially empiric and are based on experimentation or the trial-and-error method, therefore it cannot provide for all possible situations or anticipate all possible abuses. There may be crudities and inequities in complicated experimental economic legislation, but on that account alone it cannot be struck down as invalid. The decision of the Hon'ble Supreme Court to strike down only the Section 17 of the SARFAESI Act, not the entire Act, is a classic example of such self-restraint.

All the economic players in society, including the banking institutions, are empowered and constrained by the Indian Constitution. All the acts, rules and regulations must therefore be tested by the parameters given in the Constitution. "Be howsoever high, the law is above you" is its signature tune. Judicial review is essential to the growth of economic legislations in our country. It must be ensured that those implementing the law adhere to the Constitution and the laws made by Parliament. Otherwise, the rule of law is reduced to mere *ipse dixit* of the executive.

The enactment of the SARFAESI Act has wide ramification on the various systems of our country. The systems can be grouped into the following categories:

(1) Social system
(2) Legal system
(3) Banking system

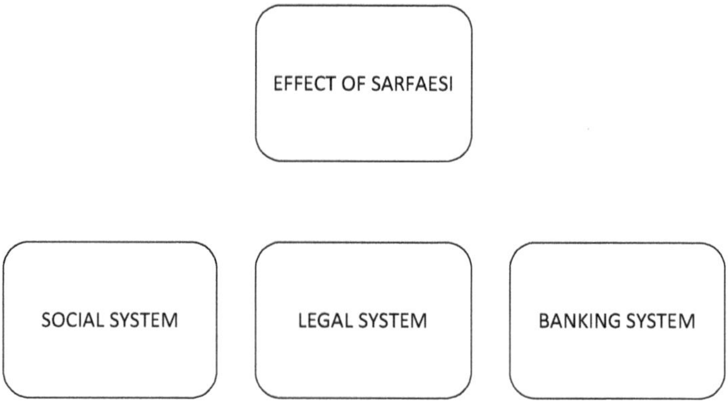

Figure 8.1 Pictorial representation of the effects of the SARFAESI Act on various systems

The effects of the SARFAESI Act on the various aforementioned systems are described pictorially in Figure 8.1.

The enactment of the SARFAESI Act has implications on the social system, legal system and banking system. The enforcement of the provisions of the SARFAESI Act has affected the social status of the borrowers and guarantors in various ways. The publication of the notices under the SARFAESI Act has adversely affected the social status of the borrowers and guarantors and also hampered their prospects of taking any further credit facilities from the banking system. The enactment of the SARFAESI Act has played pivotal role in the history of Indian jurisprudence. It is true that the enactment of the SARFAESI Act has opened a new era in legal history. However, it is equally important to note that the critics termed the Act a "draconian act". The enactment of the SARFAESI Act opened new vistas of recovery for the banks and financial institutions. The detailed effects of the SARFAESI Act on the social system are shown in Figure 8.2.

I. The effects on the social system

The proceedings under the SARFAESI Act required the publication of the names of default borrowers/guarantors. The proceedings under the SARFAESI Act are initiated by issuing the demand notice under the provisions of Section 13 (2) of the SARFAESI Act. The notice under Section 13(2) of the Act needs to be served to the borrower/guarantor and in cases of non-receipt/refusal of the notice by the borrower/guarantor, substituted service has to be instituted. The substituted service means the publication of the notice in two leading newspapers, one in vernacular language. After 60 days from the date of notice, the authorised officer of the bank can take possession of the property mortgaged/hypothecated by delivering the possession notice to the borrower/guarantor issued under Section 13(4) of the Act. Along with serving the notice, the possession notice needs to be published in two newspapers, one in the vernacular language, within 7 days from the date of taking possession. The possession notices also need to be posted to the property. Thereafter, the sale notice also needs to serve on the borrower/guarantor, published in two newspapers and affixed on the property.

The social implications of these proceedings are that the name of the borrower and details of the property are published in the public domain, and the public learns about the default committed by the borrower/guarantor; those interested in purchasing the property can submit their bid application and participate in the auction. The social stigma associated with the publication of their name and details of the property acts as a deterrent to the people who have availed themselves of the credit facilities from the bank. The social status of the borrowers who have defaulted in repayment will be damaged when their name and the details of their property are published in newspaper. The right-thinking people will view the default borrowers with suspicion and doubt and this will affect the financial integrity and borrowing capacity of defaulters.

In this context, the arbitrary exercise of powers by the banks under the SARFAESI Act will cause irreparable social damage to the borrowers and will pull down his social status among the right-thinking persons. To avoid the occurrence of such events, more caution and care on the part of the authorised officers who are exercising the powers under the SARFAESI Act is required.

The powers given to the authorized officers of the banks under Section 13(4) of the SARFAESI Act to take possession of the property are creating a fear psychosis among the borrowers. The taking of actual physical possession of the property by the banks through the authorised officers will lead to dragging the borrowers/guarantors from their property and leaving them virtually homeless. The mental state of the borrowers/guarantors, who have been driven away from the property, is highly shocking. However, it is to be remembered that in order to facilitate the sale of the property for the recovery of the dues, taking physical possession is required. The larger interest to recover public money for disbursement to the needy people will definitely override the difficulties and sufferings of the borrowers/guarantors.

The sale of property under the SARFAESI Act for a price less than the prevailing market price is a concern deeply shared by the borrowers/guarantors. The banks need to be very careful while selling the property under auction. It should be the endeavour of bankers to ensure that fixation of the reserve price is fair and transparent. If the bankers are not careful, this may amount to selling the property of borrowers/guarantors at throwaway prices. Further, the arbitrariness on the part of authorised officers may amount to irreparable loss to the borrowers/guarantors.

The lack of awareness regarding the legal remedies available under the provisions of the SARFAESI Act among the common persons especially among the borrowers/guarantors is causing lot of damage, which ultimately results in loss of right over the mortgaged property. The persons who are illiterate and uneducated are the victims of the arbitrariness of the bankers. In the study, it is found that in many cases, the care and caution which are required as per the provisions of the Act are not being followed by the authorised officers, which results in the violation of the rights of the borrowers and guarantors. The lack of transparency and maturity on the part of the authorised officers has resulted in serious difficulties to the genuine borrowers and guarantors. However, the actions of the authorised officers against the willful defaulters and fraudsters act as a deterrent force. The proceedings under the SARFAESI Act are a warning signal to all borrowers and guarantors who intend to defraud the banks and financial institutions. The Pictorial representation of the effects of the SARFAESI Act on the social system is shown in Figure 8.2.

Figure 8.2 Pictorial representation of the effects of the SARFAESI Act on the social system

II. The effects on the legal system

The judgement of the Hon'ble Supreme Court in Mardia Chemicals[1] had a profound impact on the legal system. The legal proceedings post Mardia Chemicals have given a new dimension to the recovery process. On the one hand, this judgement armed the banks with the power to take possession of the secured asset and sell it thereafter for recovery of dues. On the other hand, it enabled the aggrieved borrowers to approach the Debt Recovery Tribunal for redressal of their grievances.

The provisions of the SARFAESI Act proceedings are non-adjudicatory and non-judicial. This called for strict compliance of the provisions of the Act in letter and spirit. In terms of Rule 8 of the Enforcement of Security Interest Rules, 30-days sale notice is required to be given to the borrower/guarantor before conducting a sale/auction of the secured asset. In regard to the first auction, there is not contra-opinion that a sale notice of 30 days needs to be given to the borrower/guarantors. However, regarding the second sale notice, the High Courts vary in their view, and few High Courts have taken a stand that for the second sale notice there is no need to give 30 days. The SARFAESI Act has been amended now and only 15 days notice is required to be given for second sale.

The judgement of the Supreme Court in *Transcore v. Union of India* created far reaching consequences on the recovery proceedings initiated by banks for recovery of money. This judgement has given liberty to banks to simultaneously proceed both under the SARFAESI Act and under the RDDBFI Act. Although from the standpoint of borrowers/guarantors, it is a judgement which puts the borrowers and guarantors under the pressure of multiple legal proceedings, it has helped the bankers to initiate multiple proceedings for recovery of money.

The various judgements of the High Courts in interfering the appellate jurisdiction under the SARFAESI Act have been a serious concern of the Hon'ble Supreme Court. The judgements of various courts agreed upon the common principle that enforcement of the SARFAESI Act in compliance with the provisions of the Act are legally valid, but those actions which violate the provisions of the Act shall be struck down. The Pictorial representation of the effects of the SARFAESI Act on the legal system is shown in Figure 8.3.

III. The effects on the banking system

The introduction of the SARFAESI Act into Indian jurisprudence has been a big game changer as far the procedures pertaining to the recovery of debts are concerned. From the point of view of bankers, it rejuvenates the debt recovery procedures because prior to the Act resorting to the order of the courts was the only remedy available to them. So, in that sense, the SARFAESI Act has delivered positive results for the banks and bankers. Post the judgement of the Supreme Court in the Mardia Chemicals case, the SARFAESI Act as such doesn't contain any provisions, which is contrary to the spirit of the Indian Constitution and against the principles of natural justice. There are issues pertaining to the execution of the provisions of the SARFAESI Act which need to be improved for better protections for the genuine borrowers and guarantors.

The enforcement of the SARFAESI Act has had a profound impact on the banking system. It empowered bankers to take possession and sell the secured asset for the recovery of dues. It enabled bankers to enforce the securities without going to the court or without undergoing the tedious legal procedures. It is true that after enforcement of secured asset through the SARFAESI proceedings by the bankers, the quantum of recovery has increased many folds. It has expedited the recovery proceedings. The banks were able to save time and energy in recovery proceedings. Though the interference of the civil courts was excluded from the adjudication of the SARFAESI

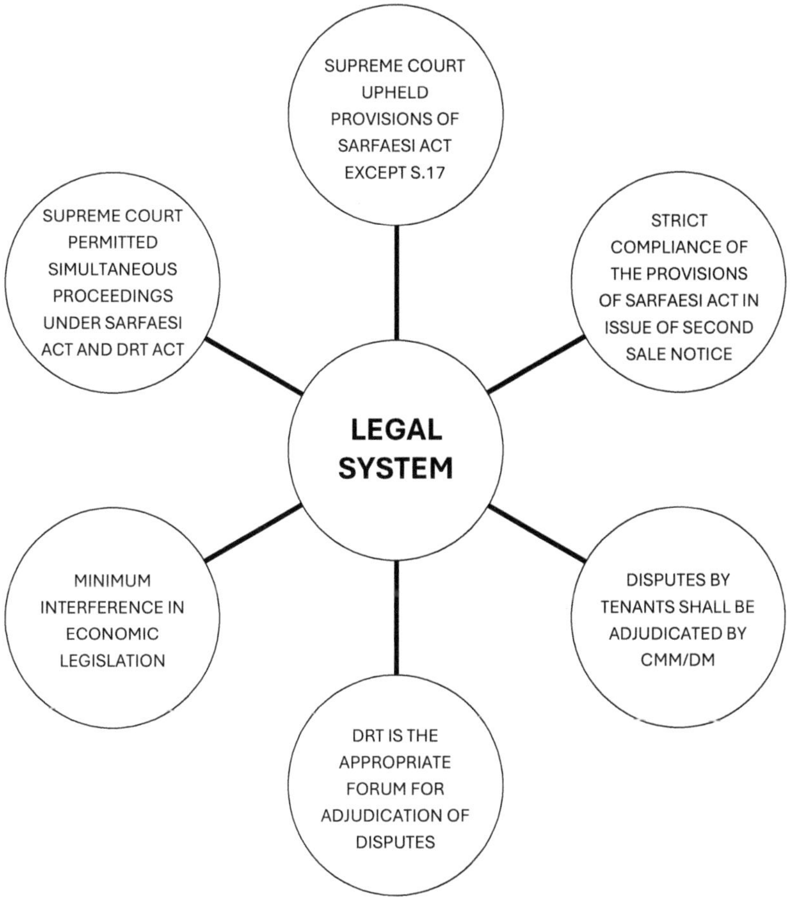

Figure 8.3 Pictorial representation of the effects of the SARFAESI Act on the legal system

proceedings, the stay granted by Debt Recovery Tribunals has delayed the SARFAESI proceedings.

From a banker's perspective, the SARFAESI Act has more gain than the pain in the matter of litigation. However, looking from the borrower's/guarantor's point of view, the SARFAESI Act proves to be ineffective in protecting their interest. On examination of the feedback from the borrowers/guarantors and other stakeholders, the proceedings under the SARFAESI Act came as a blow to them. Many instances are on record that demonstrate the abuse of the process of the SARFAESI proceedings, such as taking possession or selling a secured asset without serving proper notice on the borrower/guarantor, etc. The arbitrary and abusive use of powers by the authorised officers have invited bitter remarks from the general public and regulators and also from courts.

The effect of the SARFAESI Act on the banking legal jurisprudence can be summarised as follows:

(1) The SARFAESI Act has developed a new dimension in the interpretation of quasi-judicial legislation. The doctrine of election was tested while analysing the provisions of the SARFAESI Act, and the Hon'ble Supreme Court upheld that simultaneous proceedings under the DRT Act and the SARFAESI Act are permissible for recovering the dues of the banks.
(2) The SARFAESI Act has created a momentum in execution of the laws for the recovery of dues to banks. It empowered the banks to directly enforce the securities created in their favour without going to the court and obtaining an order/judgement.
(3) The SARFAESI Act has made the enforcement of the securities in favour of the banks easier, fast and hassle free.
(4) The enforcement of the SARFAESI Act has run into difficulties due to the arbitrary use of powers by the authorised officers of banks who lack expertise and knowledge of the provisions of the Act.
(5) Instances of violations of the rights of the borrowers and guarantors have also come to light during the enforcement of the provisions of the SARFAESI Act.
(6) The violation of the principles of natural justice led to the filings of numerous applications under Section 17 of the SARFAESI Act before tribunals and High Courts.

The efficacy of the provisions of the laws relating to the recovery of dues to banks have been tested at various judicial forums, and remedial measures to improve the efficiency of the provisions have been taken by Parliament by enacting various amendments to the Act. The important judgements by various courts have also helped to uphold the rights of deprived borrowers and guarantors who have been harmed by the unjust and unlawful acts of the authorised officers not in compliance with the true spirit of the law.

The striking down of Section 17 of the SARFAESI Act by the Hon'ble Supreme Court of India in the Mardia Chemicals case was a classic example of the arbitrary provisions of the Act that were primarily enacted for accelerating the proceedings for the recovery of dues to banks. The judgement of the Hon'ble Supreme Court in the Mardia Chemicals case was an eye opener for those who vehemently argue for a law which has stringent provisions for recovery of bank's dues. This judgement reminds us of the necessity to practice the principle of natural justice while enforcing the provisions of the SARFAESI Act. The Pictorial representation of the effects of the SARFAESI Act on the banking system is shown in Figure 8.4.

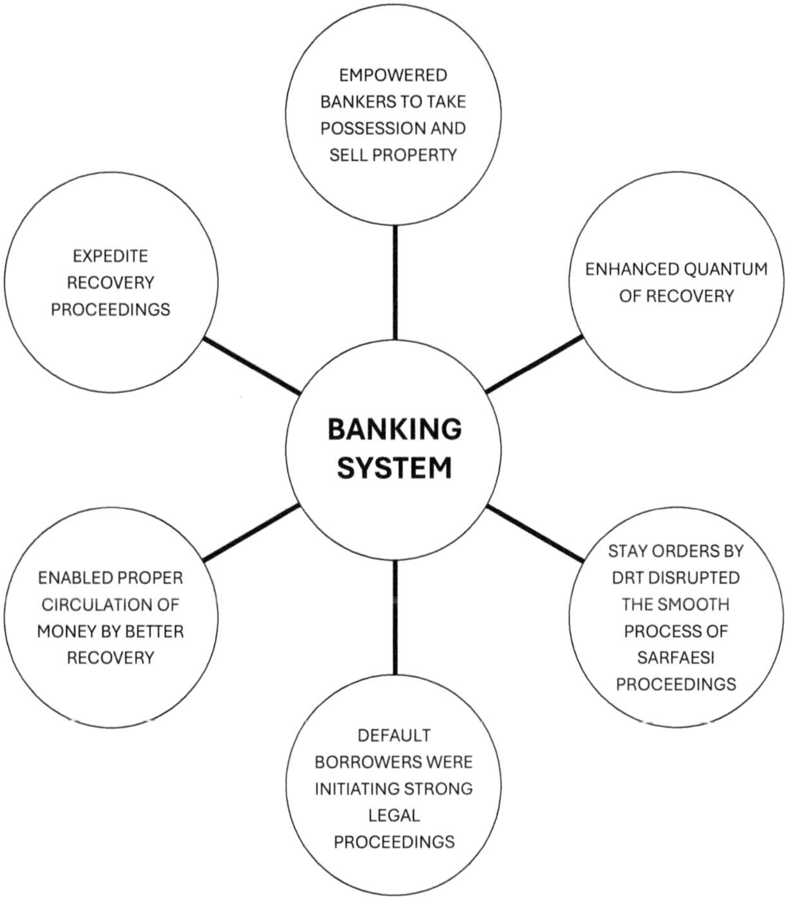

Figure 8.4 Pictorial representation of the effects of the SARFAESI Act on the banking system

Note

1 *Mardia Chemicals Ltd v. Union of India & Others* reported in 2004 D.R.T.C 1(SC).

Bibliography

Primary sources

1. The Securitisation and Reconstruction of Financial Assets and Enforcement of Security Interest Act, 2002.
2. The Recovery of Debts Due to Banks and Financial Institutions Act, 1993.
3. The Enforcement of Security Interest and Recovery of Debts Laws (Amendment) Act, 2004.
4. The Enforcement of Security Interest and Recovery of Debts Laws (Amendment) Act, 2012.
5. The Enforcement of Security Interest and Recovery of Debts Laws and Miscellaneous Provisions (Amendment) Act, 2016.
6. The Factoring Regulation Act, 2011.
7. The Bankers' Books Evidence Act, 1879.
8. The Bankers' Books Evidence Act, 1891.
9. The Banking (Acquisition and Transfer of Undertakings) Act, 1970.
10. The Banking (Acquisition and Transfer of Undertakings) Act, 1980.
11. The Banking Ombudsman Schemes, 1843.
12. The Bankruptcy Act, 1914.
13. The Companies Act, 1948.
14. The Companies Act, 2013.
15. The Consumer Protection Act, 1986.
16. The Contract Act, 1872.
17. The Credit Guarantee Corporation Act, 1961.
18. The Deposit Insurance and Credit Guarantee Corporation Act, 1961.
19. The Enforcement of Security Interest Act, 2002.
20. The Evidence Act, 1842.
21. The Foreign Exchange Management Act, 1999.
22. The General Clauses Act, 1897.
23. The Interest Act, 1878.
24. The Kerala Revenue Recovery Act, 1968.
25. The Kerala State Legal Services Authorities Act, 1987.
26. The Limitation Act, 1908; Registration Act, 1908.
27. The Income Tax Act, 1961.
28. The Arbitration and Conciliation Act, 1996.
29. The Credit Information Companies (Regulation) Act, 2005.
30. The Depositories Act, 1996.
31. Hire-Purchase Act, 1972.

32. Negotiable Instruments Act, 1881.
33. Reserve Bank of India Act, 1934.
34. Right to Information Act, 2005.
35. Sick Industrial Companies (Special Provisions) Act, 1985.
36. Specific Relief Act, 1963.
37. Stamp Act, 1899.
38. State Bank of India Act, 1955.
39. Transfer of Property Act, 1882.
40. Code of Civil Procedure, 1908.
41. Code of Criminal Procedure, 1973.
42. Constitution of India.

Rules

1. Security Interest (Enforcement) Rules, 2002.
2. Debts Recovery Tribunal (Financial and Administrative Power) Rules, 1997.
3. Debts Recovery Appellate Tribunal (Procedure) Rules, 1994.
4. Debts Recovery Tribunal (Procedure) Rules, 1993.
5. Debts Recovery Appellate Tribunal (Financial and Administrative Power) Rules, 1997.
6. Debts Recovery Tribunal (Procedure for Appointment as Presiding Officer of the Tribunal) Rules, 1998.
7. Debts Recovery Appellate Tribunal (Procedure for Appointment as Chairperson of the Appellate Tribunal) Rules, 1998.
8. Debts Recovery Tribunal (Procedure for Investigation of Misbehavior or incapacity of Presiding Officer) Rules, 2010.
9. Registration of Assignment of Reccivablcs Rulcs, 2012.
10. Debt Recovery Tribunals (Refund of Court Fee) Rules, 2013.

Secondary sources

Books

1. Justice A.B. Srivastava (2009) 6th Edition. Securitisation & Debt Recovery Laws along with Allied Acts & Rules: Law Publishers (India) Pvt. Ltd.
2. M.R. Umarji (2014) 6th Edition. Law & Practice Relating to Securitisation & Reconstruction of Financial Assets & Enforcement of Security Interest: Taxmann.
3. S.N. Gupta (2010) 5th Edition in 3 Volumes. The Banking Law in Theory & Practice: Universal Law Publishing Co.
4. M.J. Aslam (2010) 1st Edition. Legal Aspects of Bank Lending: Asia Law House.
5. U.N. Mitra (2009) 12th Edition in 2 Volumes. The Law of Limitation and Prescription: LexisNexis Butterworths Wadhwa Nagpur.
6. R. Suseelan & A.R. Anilkumar (2002) 2nd Edition. The Code of Civil Procedure, 1908: Swamy Law House.
7. G.C.V. Subha Rao (2007) 5th Edition in 2 Volumes. The Law of Transfer of Property: ALT Publications.
8. S.K. Sarkar (2010) 2nd Edition. Law Relating to Lok Adalats and Legal Aid: Orient Publishing Company.
9. Aravind Menon (2011) 1st Edition. The eLaws: Swamy Law House.
10. Sanjiva Row (2011) 11th Edition. Commentary on Law Relating to Contract Act, 1872 and Tenders: Delhi Law House.

11. Rashbehary Ghose (2010) 9th Edition. Tagore Law Lectures on Law of Mortgage: Kamal Law House.
12. B.R. Sharma (2009) 3rd Edition. Bank Frauds Prevention & Detection: Universal Law Publishing Co. Pvt. Ltd.
13. M.R. Umarji (2006) 4th Edition. Law & Practice Relating to Securitisation & Reconstruction of Financial Assets & Enforcement of Security Interest: Taxmann's.

Articles and journals

1. The Hindu: Business Line. Published on November 22, 2013: SARFAESI Act most effective tool to recover bad loans: http://www.thehindubusinessline.com.
2. The Telegraph. Published on November 26, 2014: Worry over poor loan recovery: https://groups.google.com/group/banknews.
3. The Press Trust of India. Published on November 25, 2014: Defaulting large borrowers are like freeloaders: Rajan: https://groups.google.com/group/banknews.
4. The Mint. Published on July 31, 2014: FM sets up panel to give more teeth to debt recovery laws: https://groups.google.com/group/banknews.
5. Tamal Bandyopadhyay: The Mint. Published on September 22, 2014: We need bankruptcy law to tackle defaulters: https://groups.google.com/group/banknews.
6. Vrishti Beniwal: The Business Standard. Published on August 12, 2014: Government mulls law to give banks more muscle: https://groups.google.com/group/banknews.
7. Gireesh Chandra Prasad & S. Arun: The Financial Express. Published on August 5, 2014: SARFAESI Act creditors may be allowed to exercise first right over assets: https://groups.google.com/group/banknews.
8. M. R. Umarji: The Economic Times. Published on July 2, 2014: Recovery of non-performing assets: https://groups.google.com/group/banknews.
9. Reserve Bank of India: Master Circular. Prudential norms on income recognition, asset classification and provisioning pertaining to advances: http://www.rbi.org.in.
10. S. Arun: The Financial Express. Published on April 17, 2014: Increase usage of SARFAESI Act to recover NPA: https://groups.google.com/group/banknew.
11. Satyanarayan Iyer: The Business Line. Published on March 13, 2014: In a hurry to recover loans, Banks ignore the rules of the game: https://groups.google.com/group/banknews.
12. M. J. Antony: The Business Standard. Published on August 15, 2012: Creditors in a domineering role: https://www.business-standard.com.

Reports

1. Report of the Central Board of Directors on the Working of the Reserve Bank of India for the Year Ended June 30, 2014, Submitted to the Central Government in Terms of Section 53(2) of the Reserve Bank of India Act, 1934.
2. Financial Sector Legislative Reforms Committee Report (FSLRC).
3. Financial Stability Report Issue No. 9 Reserve Bank of India.
4. A Comparative Study of Non-Performing Assets in India in the Global Context – Similarities and Dissimilarities, Remedial Measures. A Paper by Prashanth K. Reddy the Indian Institute of Management Ahmedabad, India.
5. Narasimham, M. (1998). Report of the Committee on Banking Sector Reform. Mumbai: Reserve Bank of India.

Other sources

1. List of Public Financial Institutions Notified by Central Government under Section 4A of the Companies Act, 1956.
2. Master Circular-Prudential Norms on Income Recognition, Asset Classification and Provisioning Pertaining to Advances.
3. RBI Framework for Revitalising Distressed Assets in the Economy.
4. RBI Framework for Revitalising Distressed Assets in the Economy – Refinancing of Project Loans, Sale of NPA and Other Regulatory Measures.
5. Housing Finance Companies (NHB) Directions, 2010.
6. Master Circular on Wilful Directors.
7. Prudential Guidelines on Restructuring of Advances by Banks.
8. Guidelines on Declaration of Net Asset Value of Security Receipts Issued by Securitisation Company/Reconstruction Company.
9. The Securitisation Companies and Reconstruction Companies (Reserve Bank) Guidelines and Directions, 2003 – Amendments.
10. Chaitanya, V. Krishna (2004). Causes of Non-Performing Assets in Public Sector Banks. *Economic Research*, 17 (1): 16–30.
11. Chakravarty, S. (1985). *Report of the Committee to Review the Working of the Monetary System*, Mumbai: Reserve Bank of India.
12. Mor, N. and B. Sharma (2003). *Rooting out Non-Performing Assets*, Paper Presented at the 5th Annual Conference on Money and Finance in the Indian Economy, at IGIDR, Mumbai.
13. Rakaraman, I., S. Bhaoumik and N. Bhatia (1999). NPA Variations Across Indian Commercial Banks: Some Findings. *Economic and Political Weekly*, 34 (3/4): 161–168.
14. Rajeev, M. and H. P. Mahesh (2007). Assets as Liabilities: Non Performing Assets in Commercial Banks of India. *Research Monitor, Global Development Network*, 3: 17–19.

Webliography

1. www.iba.org.in (Indian Bank's Association)/Bankers Fair Practice Code, 2004.
2. www.rbi.org.in (Reserve Bank of India)/The Banking Codes and Standard Board of India (BCSBI).
3. Finmin.nic.in (Ministry of Finance)/Financial Sector Legislative Reform Commission (FSLRC)/Report/Volumes I, II.
4. www.treasury.gov (Departmental of the Treasury)/The American Recovery and Reinvestment Act of 2009 (Recovery Act).
5. www.eulerhermes.com/court (Proceedings for Recovery of Dues in the United Kingdom)/Law of England and Wales/Laws of Scotland/Laws of Northern Ireland.
6. www.theguardian.com/Banks Exploiting Obscure Law to Raid Accounts and Recover Debts.
7. www.french-property.com/Debt Recovery Disputes in France.
8. www.gov.ukgovernment/Direct Recovery of Debts.
9. www.cedarfinancial.com/International Debt Collection for China.
10. indiancorporatelaws.blogspot.in/RBI Guidelines & SARFAESI Proceedings.
11. bankdrt.net/Appeal to DRT under SARFAESI Act to be Charged as per DRT Rules.
12. articles.economictimes.indiatimes.com/Budget 2014: Government to Set Up Additional Six New Debt Recovery Tribunals.

13. www.bu.edu/Legal Reform and Loan Repayment: The Micro Economic Impact of Debt Recovery Tribunals in India-Sujata Visaria, Boston University, April 2006.
14. www.financialexpress.com/SC Upholds Changes in SARFAESI Act.
15. www.manupatrafast.com/"As is where is Basis"/Judicial Interpretation under SARFAESI Act, 2002/R. Srinivasan.
16. www.academia.edu/Implementation of SARFAESI Act-Some Issues/International Journal of Management and Social Sciences Research (IJMSSR)/Volume 2, No. 1, January 2013.
17. www.ifmr.co.in/Why is the SARFAESI Act of Critical Importance to Lenders.
18. vinodkothari.com/Update SARFAESI Rulings.
19. www.alvarezandmarsal.com/Outlook for Stressed Assets Market in India, 2014.
20. ifrogs.org/Steps and Challenges in Insolvency Law Proceedings: Learning from Case Law.
21. www.bis.org/Problem Loan Management & MSME Financing/R. Gandhi, Deputy Governor, RBI.
22. lawstreetindia.com.
23. www.assocham.org/Reports of Annual Conference.
24. articles.economictimes.indiatimes.com/What to Do if You Can't Pay Your Home Loan EMI.
25. pezzottaitejournals.net/Major Issues in Non-Performing Assets of Commercial Branch in India/International Journal of Applied Financial Management Perspectives (c) Pezzottaite Journals/Volume 2, pp. 527–536, November 3, July–September, 2013.
26. www.halsburys.in/Enforcement of Security Interest Rights of Secured Creditors Inter se.
27. www.caclubindia.com/Tenancy Rights and Action under SARFAESI Act, 2002.
28. en.wikipedia.org/Narasimhan Committee on Banking Sector Reforms (1998)/ Narasimhan Committee Report on the Financial System, 1991.
29. www.business-standard.com/Sale Notices by Banks More Visible as Borrowers under Stress: Assocham.
30. www.business-standard.com/What is the SARFAESI Act.
31. www.business-standard.com/Co-op Banks Can't Use SARFAESI for Debt Recovery: Gujarat HC.
32. www.business-standard.com/NBFCs Demand Recovery Powers, Tax Benefits Like Banks.
33. www.business-standard.com/Letters: Banking on the SARFAESI Act.
34. www.business-standard.com/M. J. Antony: Creditors in a Domineering rolewww. thehindubusinessline.com/FinMin Pushes for Computerization of Debt Recovery Tribunals.
35. https://blog.ipleaders.in/overview-of-the-SARFAESI-axt-2002/Overview of the SARFAESI Act, 2002.
36. https://ibclaw.in/critical-analysis-of-the-mandatory-issuance-of-notices-under-rule-8-and-rule-9-of-the-security-interest-enforcement-rules-2002.
37. Reserve Bank of India – Master Circulars (rbi.org.in) Notification as Amended up to June 30, 2015 – The Securitisation Companies and Reconstruction Companies (Reserve Bank) Guidelines and Directions, 2003.
38. cleartax.in/SARFAESI ACT, 2002 – Applicability, Objectives, Process, Documentation.
39. visheshupadhyay.com/SARFAESI Act Explained with Infographics.
40. lawyersclubindia.com/SARFAESI & DRT: Few Important Issues under SARFAESI Act, 2002.

41. Enforcement of Security Interest under SARFAESI (The Securitisation and Reconstruction of Financial Assets and Enforcement of Security Interest) Act 2002 – Law Times Journal Enforcement of Security Interest under SARFAESI.
42. reedlaw.in/Sections 73 and 74 of the Indian Contract Act Do Not Apply to the Forfeiture of Earnest Money under Rule 9(5) of the SARFAESI Rules.
43. https://bankingschool.co.in/loans-and-advances/recovery-through-SARFAESI-act-2002/Full Details of the Recovery Process through SARFAESI Act, 2002.
44. https://www.lawyersclubindia.com/articles/Publication-of-statutory-notices-in-two-leading-newspapers-Security-Interest-Enforcement-Rules-4986.asp.
45. mondaq.com/India – Securitization & Structured Finance – Rights of Secured Creditors Under SARFAESI – How Protected are the Rights?
46. https://www.eauctionsindia.com/blogs/rights-of-auction-purchaser-under-SARFAESI-actRights of Auction Purchaser under SARFAESI Act.
47. https://www.lawyersclubindia.com/articles/Valuation-of-secured-assets-the-procedure-and-practice-under-SARFAESI-Act-2002–5206.asp.
48. https://taxguru.in/corporate-law/highlights-of-SARFAESI-act-2002.html.

Index

Page numbers in *italic* indicate a figure and page numbers in **bold** indicate a table on the corresponding page.

adjudicatory forum, non-availability of 39–41
administrator, appointment of 69
Andhyarujina Committee 3, 13, 23
appeal: to Debt Recovery Tribunal (DRT) 67; provision 39
appellate proceedings 32–33
arbitrary powers to banks 37
assets, non-performing *see* non-performing assets (NPAs)
authorised officer: approaching CMM/DM before taking possession of property 112–113; fair play and 109–110; good faith and 109–110
authority of Tribunals 48–49

banking system: effects of SARFAESI Act on 130–133, *133*
BIFR *see* Board for Industrial and Financial Reconstruction (BIFR)
Board for Industrial and Financial Reconstruction (BIFR) 118
borrower, consent of: sale of property by private treaty 115

cash credit (CC) 6, 84, 96
chief judicial magistrates: power to issue orders under Section 14 of SARFAESI Act 110–111
chief metropolitan magistrate: in taking possession of secured asset, assistance of 68
CIRP *see* Corporate Insolvency Resolution Process (CIRP)
civil court: barred, jurisdiction of 67; jurisdiction 111–112; powers of 54
CoC *see* Committee of Creditors (CoC)
commercial and judicial domains, separation of powers between 120
Committee of Creditors (CoC) 119, 121
Committee on the Financial System 2, 9
Constitution of India 4
constitutional frameworks of recovery laws: Delhi High Court judgement 16–17; Gauhati High Court judgement 17; Karnataka High Court judgement 17–18; Supreme Court of India judgement 18–23
constitutional validity of SARFAESI Act: account as NPA-legal validity, classification of 26–30; appellate proceedings 32–33; independent adjudicatory authority 35–36; Mardia Chemicals case, after effects of Supreme Court decision in 25; mechanism to resolve legal issues 30–31; public interest *vs.* private interest 34–35; representation/objection under Section 3 (3A) of SARFAESI Act, communicating reasons for rejection of 31; right to filing appeal before DRT 31–32; 75% for filing appeal, pre-deposit of 33–34
Corporate Insolvency Resolution Process (CIRP) 119, 122
credit discipline 122
creditor-in-control 117
creditors, dominant role of 118–119

debt: certificate by Tribunal, issue of 52–53; definition of 48; as non-performing asset 29, 71, 76; recovery of 2
debtor-in-possession 117

Debts Recovery Appellate Tribunals (DRAT) 11, 68; filing of appeal before 53–54
Debts Recovery Tribunals (DRT) 11, 12; appeal to 67; backlog of pending cases in 24; right to filing appeal before 31–32
decision-making process, expediting 119
directors, change of 69
district magistrate: in taking possession of secured asset, assistance of 68
DRAT *see* Debts Recovery Appellate Tribunals (DRAT)
DRT *see* Debts Recovery Tribunals (DRT)

e-auction, legal validity of 113–114
efficient managers: liberty of financial creditors to select 120
entrepreneurship 118
evolution of recovery laws 6–14; DRT stage *8*, 11–12; IBC stage *8*, 14; pre-DRT stage *8*, 11; SARFAESI stage *8*, 12–13; stages of 8–14, *8*

filing application: delay in disposal of 113; procedure for 49–50

GNPA *see* gross non-performing assets (GNPA)
going concern concept 121–122
good faith, protection of action taken in 69–70
gross non-performing assets (GNPA) 122

Housing Finance Corporations 27

IBC *see* Insolvency and Bankruptcy Code (IBC)
immovable assets, possession of 62–63; valuation of 63
immovable property, sale procedure of 65–66
Income-tax Act: application of provisions to RDB Act 58
independent adjudicatory authority 35–36
Insolvency and Bankruptcy Code (IBC) 117–124; commercial and judicial domains, separation of powers between 120; credit discipline 122; creditor-in-control 117; creditors, dominant role of 118–119; debtor-in-possession 117; decision-making process, expediting 119; efficient managers 120; entrepreneurship 118; going concern concept 121–122; judicial hands-off, recognition of 118; realistic approach 120–121; recovery in real terms 123; resolution professional, role of 122; stay orders 119–120; team effort 122; time 119

judiciary in interpreting and establishing recovery laws relating to banking institutions, role of 73–106
jurisdiction of Tribunals 48–49

legal system: effects of SARFAESI Act on 129–130, *131*
lenders liability 37–38
limitation period 61, 70
loans 6; as non-performing assets 38
Lok Adalat 70

Ministry of Finance 66; Department of Financial Services 27
movable assets, possession of 62; valuation of 63
movable property, sale procedure of 64–65

Narasimham Committee I 12, 13, 23, 29
Narasimham Committee II 3, 12
National Housing Bank 27
natural justice 7, 11, 21, 36, 39, 60, 130; Tribunal guided by 54; violation of 132
net non-performing assets (NNPA) 122
NNPA *see* net non-performing assets (NNPA)
non-adjudicatory procedures 38
non-judicial procedures 38
non-performing assets (NPAs) 1–4, 9, 12, 14, 24, 27–30, 33, 36–38, 40, 41, 47, 60, 68, 70, 74, 75, 80, 94, 95, 97–98, 123, 124; accumulation of 10; classification of account as *see* non-performing assets, classification of account as; debt as 29, 71, 76; definition of **26**, 29; gross 122; investments as 85; loan as 38; management of 117; net 122; recovery of 76, 77, 123; reduction of 71; transfer of 58

non-performing assets, classification of account as: challenges 30–31; legal validity 26–30
non-service of notice 61
notice: non-service of 61; of sale 64, 114; Section 13(2), further proceedings after expiry of 60 days in 61–62
NPAs *see* non-performing assets (NPAs)

OD *see* overdrafts (OD)
One Time Settlement 10
overdrafts (OD) 6, 29

powers of Tribunals 48–49; to appoint receivers 51; to pass interim orders 50–51
public interest *vs.* private interest 34–35

RBI *see* Reserve Bank of India (RBI)
Recovery of Debts and Bankruptcy Act, 1993 (RDB Act): authority of Tribunals 48–49; debt, definition of 48; debt certificate by Tribunal, issue of 52–53; deposit of amount of debt on filing appeal 54; filing application, procedure for 49–50; filing of appeal before DRAT 53–54; Income-tax Act, application of provisions of 58; jurisdiction of Tribunals 48–49; modes of recovery 55–57; natural justice principle, Tribunal guided by 54; powers of civil court 54; powers of Tribunals *see* powers of Tribunals; transfer of pending cases 58
Recovery of Debts Due to Banks and Financial Institutions Act, 1993: challenges faced by 23–24
recovery of dues to banks 2, 9, 10, 18, 37, 73, 74, 86, 87, 106, 109, 128–130; legislations relating to 47–72, 125, 132; modes of 55–57; right to 7; stages of 7, *7*
representation/objection: reply to 61; under Section 3 (3A) of SARFAESI Act, communicating reasons for rejection of 31
Reserve Bank of India (RBI) 10, 29; "Framework to Revitalise the Distressed Assets in the Economy" 14; guidelines 114–115; on NPA-legal validity 27; "RBIs Prudential norms on Income Recognition, Asset Classification and Provisioning Pertaining to Advances" 28, 76
resolution professional, role of 122
Revenue Recovery Act 70–71
right to filing appeal, before DRT 31–32

sale certificate, issue of 66–67
sale procedure: of immovable property 65–66; of movable property 64–65
SARFAESI Act: administrator, appointment of 69; appeal to Debt Recovery Tribunal 67; chief metropolitan magistrate/district magistrate in taking possession of secured asset, assistance of 68; civil court barred, jurisdiction of 67; constitutional validity of 4, 24–36; Debts Recovery Appellate Tribunals 68; dimensions of *59*; directors, change of 69; enactment of 12–13; exemptions 68; further proceedings after expiry of 60 days in Section 13(2) notice 61–62; good faith, protection of action taken in 69–70; immovable assets, possession of 62–63; immovable property, sale procedure of 65–66; implications of 125–133, *126*; issues and challenges in enforcing 108–115; limitation period 61, 70; movable assets, possession of 62, 63; movable property, sale procedure of 64–65; non-service of notice 61; notice of sale 64; recent development in 41–42, **42–45**; reply to representation or objection 61; sale certificate, issue of 66–67; service of notice 60–61; shortfall, recovery of 67; takeover of management, effects of 69; *see also individual entries*
secured creditor 112
service of notice 60–61
shortfall, recovery of 67
social systen: effects of SARFAESI Act on 127–128, *129*
state tenancy laws 108–109
stay orders 119–120
symbolic possession of property 90

takeover of management, effects of 69
team effort 122
Tiwari Committee 2; recommendation of 10–11
transfer of pending cases 58

For Product Safety Concerns and Information please contact our EU
representative GPSR@taylorandfrancis.com
Taylor & Francis Verlag GmbH, Kaufingerstraße 24, 80331 München, Germany

www.ingramcontent.com/pod-product-compliance
Ingram Content Group UK Ltd.
Pitfield, Milton Keynes, MK11 3LW, UK
UKHW022032061126
477531UK00003B/174

* 9 7 8 1 0 3 2 3 7 3 6 0 7 *